KEYS TO PERSONAL FINANCIAL PLANNING

Third Edition

D. Larry Crumbley, C.P.A., Cr.FA
KPMG Endowed Professor
Louisiana State University

L. Murphy Smith, C.P.A.
Professor of Accounting
Texas A&M University

BARRON'S

All inquiries should be addressed to:
Barron's Educational Series, Inc.
250 Wireless Boulevard
Hauppauge, New York 11788
http://www.barronseduc.com

International Standard Book No. 0-7641-2099-9

Library of Congress Catalog Card No. 2001052869

Library of Congress Cataloging-in-Publication Data
Crumbley, D. Larry.
    Keys to personal financial planning / D. Larry Crumbley, L. Murphy Smith.—
3rd ed.
        p.   cm.—(Barron's business keys)
    Includes index.
    ISBN 0-7641-2099-9 (alk. paper)
    1. Finance, Personal.   I. Smith, L. Murphy.   II. Title.   III. Series.
HG179 .C78 2002
332.024—dc21

                                                                                2001052869

PRINTED IN THE UNITED STATES OF AMERICA

9 8 7 6 5 4 3 2 1

Dedication
For Donna. Thanks for everything.—DLC
For Mary Katherine,
my faithful wife and soul mate.—LMS

About the Authors

Larry Crumbley

Dr. D. Larry Crumbley, C.P.A., Cr.FA is the KPMG Endowed Professor of Accounting at Louisiana State University. He is one of America's most prolific authors and venerable academics. He helped organize and later served as president of the American Taxation Association. He has authored 50 books and over 300 major articles. He has published in the *The Accounting Review, National Tax Journal, Journal of the American Taxation Association, Tax Notes, Tax Law Review, The CPA Journal, Journal of Accountancy,* and *Petroleum Accounting and Financial Management Journal.* He has authored 12 novels, including *The Ultimate Rip-Off: A Taxing Tale.* Dr. Crumbley has traveled extensively to study accounting and taxation issues throughout the world, including the former Soviet Union, Europe, Australia, New Zealand, Israel, Egypt, Mexico, Canada, Asia, South and Central America, Indonesia, Africa, and Japan.

Murphy Smith

Dr. L. Murphy Smith, C.P.A. is Assistant Department Head and Professor in the Accounting Department at Texas A&M University. He also serves as the director of A&M's Internal Auditing Program. Dr. Smith previously worked as a faculty resident in the auditing area for a Big Five public accounting firm. He is a member of the American Institute of C.P.A.s, the Institute of Internal Auditors, and the American Accounting Association. Dr. Smith's accomplishments include over 300 professional journal articles, research grants, books, and professional meeting presentations in the U.S. and abroad. His work has been cited in various news media, including *Fortune, USA Today,* and *The Wall Street Journal.* Among the books he has published, his accounting information systems text is now in its third edition. His educational novel, *The Bottom Line is Betrayal,* has been described as an "instructional thriller" that provides an innovative way to present business concepts and issues to students. He serves on the editorial boards of several journals, including *Advances in International Accounting, Journal of Information Systems, Research on Accounting Ethics, Teaching Business Ethics,* and *The CPA Journal.*

CONTENTS

1

INTRODUCTION

Most Americans spend most of their lives earning money, but they rarely spend any time planning how to use their accumulated capital efficiently. When many people reach age 65 they are financially unprepared for retirement. Income from Social Security is inadequate to support people at today's rate of payment, and few observers can predict the future of Social Security.

Systematic personal financial planning (PFP) should begin as early as possible in your career. Financial planning is both a process and an attitude. PFP should become a habit. Financial planning involves gathering all your financial and emotional data, analyzing these data, and preparing a financial plan for the future. You must take action and follow the plan. Finally, you need to review the plan and make necessary changes as your environment and financial conditions change.

1. Prepare a balance sheet. The first step is to determine where you are now by preparing a balance sheet in order to determine your net worth. As John Kennedy said, "You have to know where you've been, to know where you are going." Your net worth is the excess of your assets over your liabilities. You must manage your cash in order to save some investment capital each month. A budget or cash flow statement will help you to determine your inflows and outflows. Reconciling your checkbook regularly is important for your financial security. Reconciliation helps you review your expenditures and analyze areas where you might cut back if necessary, and of course it

ensures that you and your banker agree about how much money you have spent and how much is available to you. Nonsufficient funds fees can be very costly.

2. Determine where you wish to go. Next you need to determine where you wish to go. What are your short-term and long-term goals? Seneca said that "Our plans miscarry because they have no aim. When a man does not know what harbor he is making for, no wind is the right wind." What are your objectives? To buy a new car? To educate your children? To prepare for retirement? To travel around the world?

   You must determine objectives and how you plan to reach them. These goals and objectives must be reviewed regularly. Did you meet your short-term goals? Are you progressing toward your long-term goals?

3. Prepare a plan to reach your goals. Once you know your objectives, you now must prepare a plan or a roadmap for reaching them. Preparing a financial plan resembles doing a jigsaw puzzle in that many pieces must be put together to get a completed puzzle. These pieces or variables include budgeting, recordkeeping, tax planning, planning for inflation, selecting competent advisors, buying insurance, investing your capital, planning for education and retirement, and estate planning. Some of these financial planning puzzle pieces are constantly changing shape, especially those affected by tax law. Tax laws can literally change overnight, by the actions of Congress. Any tax-related information in this book should be double-checked against the most current tax law.

4. Know your obstacles. Although you, like many people, may have an overall goal of accumulating wealth, you must understand that there are many obstacles in your way. Among these are inflation,

taxes, limited number of working hours, recessions, unemployment, injuries, procrastination, and dishonest sellers—the list goes on. But you should realize that there are ways to accumulate real wealth. You may review the ways that are offered in our book, and understand the annuity concept, leveraging, and employing people to work for you.

This book does not promote a get-rich-quick strategy. It does not offer a mishmash of euphemisms, hyperbole, and stirring testimonials. In fact, you should avoid the fast-buck ads that offer you a short road to riches. Consumers spend an estimated $60 million annually responding to offers of instant wealth. These "fantastic money-making plans" are often typo-laden, poorly written books or pamphlets that propose a variety of outlandish schemes for getting rich through real estate, mail-order sales, or telemarketing. These get-rich-quick promoters understand the rule about a fool and his money. Contrary to promoters' claims, success, and wealth are usually not obtained either quickly or easily. We follow Mark Twain's advice about speculation. There are two times when you should not speculate: when you cannot afford to and when you can.

Making wise investments is a process that requires specialized knowledge and careful planning. Picking the right advisors is not easy. You need to understand basic financial concepts; the concept of risk versus return is basic to any investment strategy. How safe is your principal? Diversification, dollar cost averaging, a parking lot for your idle funds, mutual funds, liquidity, and the umbrella of insurance are terms that you must understand.

Do not wait too long to begin your retirement and estate planning. There are numerous aspects to consider. As you plan for retirement, are you socking away some of your monthly earnings into an Individual Retirement

Account, a 401(k) plan, a Keogh plan, a defined contribution plan, or some other pension or profit-sharing plan? A small increase in your investment return inside a retirement plan can result in tremendous benefits at your retirement. Estate planning is really building an estate during your lifetime and passing it on to your heirs in a form that minimizes income and estate taxes. A will is essential; a prenuptial agreement may be important. You may wish to consider using a trust to minimize taxes and to carry out many business and non-business objectives.

Personal financial planning is complex and time-consuming. PFP can be frustrating. Financial planning may not make you wealthy. You may never appear on "Lifestyles of the Rich and Famous." However, lack of planning is equivalent to planning for failure. Planning will almost certainly result in your being better off than if you had not planned and will, we hope, result in your life being fuller and happier. As rags-to-riches George Shinn, owner of the National Basketball Association's Charlotte Hornets, has said, "I would rather fail doing something than make a mistake of doing nothing." Your financial success is worth some time and effort. Plan today for your financial well-being.

2

DETERMINING NET WORTH: WHERE ARE YOU?

The purpose of preparing a personal balance sheet is to determine how much money you now have, so you can then estimate how much more you will need to reach your short-term and long-term financial goals. The short-term goals will be more directly connected to your current situation. For example, if your monthly expenses exceed your monthly income, then one of your short-term goals should be to reverse that situation, either by reducing expenses or increasing income.

Preparation of a personal balance sheet will enable you to identify what you own (your assets) and what you owe (your liabilities). Assets are listed in order of liquidity, and liabilities are listed in order of claim. The difference between the two, assets minus liabilities, is your net worth. Several other terms that you need to know in order to properly complete and analyze your personal balance sheet include the following: (1) fixed assets, (2) appreciating assets, (3) diversification, (4) portfolio, and (5) return on portfolio.

Fixed assets are assets that depreciate in value. In other words, they decrease in value over their lifetime.

Appreciating assets are assets that have the possibility of increasing in value over their lifetime.

Diversification is allocating your money among many different types of assets rather than concentrating them in one asset. Diversification reduces the danger that you will lose the overall value of your investments.

Portfolio of assets includes all the assets you possess.

The return on your portfolio includes both the cash generated from your investments and the annual increase in the fair market value of investment instruments, such as stocks and bonds.

A sample personal balance sheet form is provided in Exhibit 2.1. Assets are basically those things that you own or will eventually own once they are paid for. Examples of most common types of assets, as shown, include cash, house, stocks, bonds, and cars.

Liquidity refers to how easily an asset can be converted into cash. Personal assets, such as a house or car, are much less liquid than stocks or bonds. In other words, the less liquid an asset is, the longer it usually takes to sell and thus provide you with its market value in cash. A good idea is to evaluate whether your assets are those that you believe will appreciate in value or those that won't. There is an obvious advantage in having assets that will go up in value as opposed to having assets that will either maintain or decrease in value. A house is often considered an appreciating asset, but today it may either maintain its value or decrease in value (see Key 21).

Liabilities are items that represent a future outlay of cash. Exhibit 2.1 lists some of the more common liabilities. Don't forget to include liabilities connected to assets on which you still owe money. For instance, you might still owe half the value of your auto. In this situation, include the unpaid portion of your auto loan (the part you are still paying off) under car loans in the liability section of your personal balance sheet and the fair market value of the car in the asset section.

Once you have totaled your assets and liabilities, you are ready to calculate your net worth by subtracting total liabilities from total assets. Your net worth is a snapshot of your financial standing at a particular point in time.

By comparing your yearly snapshots, you'll be able to determine your financial progress.

After preparing your personal balance sheet, you should consider the composition of your individual assets and liabilities. Are your assets made up of clothes, furniture, or other depreciating assets? Wouldn't you be better off if you acquired assets that are likely to appreciate, such as stocks or real estate? However, if you invest only in real estate and real estate values decrease, then your assets lose money instead of appreciating. The way to reduce the risk that your assets won't appreciate is to have several different types of appreciating assets. You need to diversify. If one type of asset doesn't go up in value, perhaps another type of asset will.

After computing your personal net worth, you have a good idea of your present financial condition. Are you satisfied or dissatisfied with your present condition? In either case, knowing where you are enables you to make plans for the future. If your personal net worth is a negative amount, then your top-priority financial goal should be to pay off some debts (see Key 3). If your net worth is only a small positive number—that is, assets barely exceeding liabilities—then a financial emergency could put you in a precarious situation. A primary financial goal should be to increase your net worth by either decreasing your liabilities, increasing your appreciating assets, or both.

The next key discusses setting goals and financial objectives.

EXHIBIT 2.1
Personal Balance Sheet

Assets

Cash in bank checking account	$ _____
Other bank accounts	$ _____
Money market accounts	$ _____
House	$ _____
Cars	$ _____
Furnishings and appliances	$ _____
Clothing, jewelry, and art	$ _____
Stocks, bonds, and other securities	$ _____
Cash value of insurance and annuities	$ _____
Retirement savings, such as IRAs or employee savings plan	$ _____
Other	$ _____
TOTAL ASSETS	$ _____

Liabilities

Taxes owed	$ _____
Mortgage loans	$ _____
Alimony and/or child support owed	$ _____
Credit card debt	$ _____
Car loans	$ _____
Education loans	$ _____
Any unpaid bills	$ _____
Other debt	$ _____
TOTAL LIABILITIES	$ _____
PERSONAL NET WORTH	$ _____

(Total Assets Minus Total Liabilities)

3

SETTING GOALS AND FINANCIAL OBJECTIVES: WHERE ARE YOU GOING?

If you are like most people, one of your financial goals is to be independently wealthy. Ultimately, at some point in your life, you will probably no longer be able to work. You will then live off either your investments, pension, government transfer payments, or charity.

Wealth itself is a difficult term to define. Wealth can be defined as the amount of money necessary for personal contentment. Are you wealthy? Some people do not consider themselves wealthy even though they have millions of dollars. The amount of money necessary to be considered financially successful or independently wealthy varies greatly among individuals. Real success involves many dimensions, not just money (see Key 40). Real success includes good relations with family, friends, and colleagues. On the other hand, most people want to be a financial success. Monetary success does not usually happen overnight, but it can happen for anyone who is willing to make good plans and stick to them.

The starting point in achieving financial success is to know and accept where you are today (see Key 2). There is no use making excuses for a poor financial position if that's where you find yourself. The productive thing to do is to plan how to improve it. On the other hand, you

9

may not be in bad shape, but with proper planning you may be able to improve an already good situation. This improvement is achieved by acquiring financial knowledge and resolving to take control of your own financial future.

A lack of financial knowledge stops most people from ever changing their financial situation. Knowledge can best be obtained by reading and studying. At first, it won't be easy, but you eventually will begin to appreciate how the learning curve applies in gaining financial knowledge. To get started and to gain momentum, it may take a dozen units (for instance, hours) of effort to get one unit (for instance, $100) of positive results. People with a financial knack are not simply born with the ability. They have developed the ability over time by reading about and studying the subject of personal finances. Consequently, a financially adept person can expend one unit of effort to get a dozen times the results of other people.

Some helpful hints for improving your financial situation include the following:

1. Accept your current situation as a starting point and realize that you can change it for the better with the right kind of knowledge.
2. Realize that only you can improve your financial situation. No broker, money manager, or relative can put more effort and dedication into changing your financial situation than you can. Take control of your own financial future.
3. Read enough financial literature to feel confident about the financial decisions you have to make. Know what you're doing. Some people may get the hang of it after reading only one book. However, other people may need to read several books and to talk with several consultants before they are sure of what they are doing.
4. You are probably set in the way you spend money.

If so, then you may need to change your spending habits. This change is much easier said than done. You can easily make purchases on a credit card that charges 15 percent annual interest, even when you don't have money in the bank; waiting to make purchases until after you have accumulated the necessary funds requires discipline. You must develop budgetary discipline to succeed financially. Discipline is a good habit to have for managing any area of your life, but it is indispensable in the financial area.

After you acquire the necessary knowledge and understanding to improve your financial position, your next step is to implement the new information so that you can achieve financial success.

You should ask yourself why financial success is one of your goals. What are the objectives motivating your efforts to understand personal finance? What is the point of it all? You should establish clear goals to keep you motivated and on track. Exhibit 3.1 provides a short list of possible objectives. Each goal you select should be ranked as short-term or long-term. Those in the short-term column should be achieved first, while those in the long-term column are achieved second. You will need to achieve certain short-term goals on your way to some particular long-term achievement. Furthermore, many goals will be interrelated, such as having children and financing their education. Without stated goals, you will expend effort without a purpose. If you lack a purpose, you may wind up achieving nothing.

Acquisition of wealth begins when your monthly income exceeds expenses. At that point you can invest the excess in different financial mechanisms that earn you money. But what if your monthly expenses exceed your monthly income? What if your monthly income only barely exceeds your expenses? What if your monthly income exceeds your expenses, but you are unsure what investments to make? Each of these questions can be answered by regarding wealth acquisition as the end result of implementing three financial management approaches: budget management, tax management, and investment management. All three approaches are important, and failure to implement even one will greatly hamper wealth acquisition.

Budget management is intended to increase the difference between your monthly cash inflow and monthly cash outflow in order to have as much money as possible to invest.

Tax management helps you minimize the taxes you pay to federal, state, and local governments.

Investment management helps you to earn the maximum return on the investments made from your net cash inflow each month.

EXHIBIT 3.1
Example of Personal Goals

Possible Goals	Short-Term	Long-Term
Minimize your debt	_____	_____
Build an emergency fund	_____	_____
Buy a house	_____	_____
Make home improvements	_____	_____
Buy a vacation home	_____	_____
Buy a new car	_____	_____
Have children	_____	_____
Finance children's education	_____	_____
Buy major luxury items	_____	_____
Buy new furniture or appliances	_____	_____
Enjoy an expensive vacation	_____	_____
Take time off from work	_____	_____
Start your own business	_____	_____
Retire early	_____	_____
Live in style after retirement	_____	_____
Other	_____	_____

4

SPENDING PATTERNS

Personal spending patterns vary dramatically, chiefly because people have many different goals and objectives (see Key 3). These goals and objectives are somewhat related to demographic characteristics, such as age and educational background and personal characteristics. For example, some people are frugal, while others are swimming in a pool of mortgages, debt, and personal loans.

Baby boomers are receiving a great deal of media attention today. They are roughly the generation of people born from the late 1940s to the early 1960s. Baby boomers in their late thirties and through early fifties are the biggest spenders in the market today. Consequently, advertisers are targeting relatively more dollars at this age group than at other groups.

Education plays a key role in determining a person's spending patterns. In general, college-educated people earn more and spend more than less educated people. As a result, many consumer product companies gear their marketing to those households with college-educated inhabitants.

Similarly, people with college educations tend to invest for their future more than those who have not attended college. People without college educations generally have less money to invest after immediate needs are met. In addition, college graduates spend about twice as much on entertainment as nongraduates do. College graduates account for 60 percent of clothing sales. College graduates allocate 6 percent of their budgets to health care, compared to barely 4 percent of the less educated person's budget. College graduates spend roughly five times the amount spent on education by non college graduates.

Personal spending patterns vary tremendously among different people. Your own spending pattern is affected by many factors, including your age, your education, your household income, your personal tastes, and your stage in life (see Key 5). For example, older people spend more money on medicine, drugs, and doctors. Lower-income households spend a larger percentage of their income on food and other necessities. The percentage of spending on automotive products and services increases as income increases.

Other factors affecting your spending pattern may include your marital status, the number of children, place of residence, sex, race, moral and religious beliefs, and cultural background. Young, unmarried people spend a larger percentage of income on recreation and clothing. Family priorities shift to educational needs when children reach certain ages. Members of certain religious groups donate more earnings to their church, synagogue, or temple.

Your spending pattern will change as your financial goals and objectives change. Spending money in a way that generates the highest quality of life, given both your own desires and the money you have, is an art based on sound financial principles. Learning how to allocate your financial resources in a way that provides for a quality lifestyle now and in the future is the key to financial success. Financial success results from planning, not worrying about, the use of your financial resources. Financial success should be everyone's goal.

5

YOUR STAGE IN LIFE

Abraham Maslow, a psychologist, divided human needs into five different hierarchical levels. As he observed people, he concluded that different people were dissatisfied with life for different reasons and that these people seemed to be at different levels.

From these observations, he developed what is known as the hierarchy of needs. Everyone has many different needs important to them, but these needs seem to be organized into five different levels. A person may not strive to satisfy a need at a higher level until the lower level need has been fulfilled. At that point, an individual becomes dissatisfied with life in some way and begins to strive for something more.

Physiological needs. The first and most basic needs are the *physiological* needs: food, shelter, and clothing. Physiological needs are necessities. This stage is the first level because these items are needed to survive.

Safety needs. After people have fulfilled physiological needs, they move to the second level, *safety* needs. People wish to feel secure, stable, and safe. For some people, safety means a good, permanent job, a savings account, or life insurance. Each person has his or her own definition of safety.

Belonging and love. Physiological and safety needs are basic to everyone. After these two needs are fulfilled, the third need is for *belonging* and *love*. People want to feel loved and trusted by others.

Esteem. The fourth level in Maslow's hierarchy is *esteem* needs. People wish to be recognized and appreciated. They want to be appreciated because that makes them feel better about themselves. Popular people probably have a high self-esteem.

Self-actualization. The final level is called *self-actualization*. At this level, individuals realize that they have a talent for something, whether it is writing, drawing, or playing music, and strive for perfection within their talent.

There are, of course, other ways to describe the stages of human life. For example, the American Institute of Certified Public Accountants, concentrating on economics, points out that families fit into five stages:

- **Stage one.** Employed, before marriage. With little responsibility to others, the single person can afford to take risks. Long-term growth is one objective during this phase. Clothing and recreation are important. Insurance generally is not relevant.
- **Stage two.** Married, before children. This is a time to begin accumulating assets, despite heavy pressure to spend on other things. Careful budgeting is essential. Furnishings for the home are important. Insurance becomes a factor, although perhaps not a substantial one.
- **Stage three.** Married, precollege children. Insurance protection becomes very important. Income may increase significantly, but so does the need to spend. Budgeting becomes even more important. So does tax planning. Concern about future college costs begins.
- **Stage four.** The empty nest. Earning power may be at a peak. Risk avoidance becomes important; investment strategy tends toward building up capital. Many consider a second career. Travel may become more important.
- **Stage five.** Retirement. A steady, comfortable income is now a concern. Investment strategy must be balanced. There is greater freedom, but

risk must be limited because the time necessary to recover from a disaster is no longer there.

What stage fits you? Spending patterns differ at the various stages (see Key 4), and you need to be aware of this as you plan your budget. But you should also take note of the changes that are likely to come in the future so that you can make your long-range plans realistic. Our discussion will focus on the 30–45 age group (married with children) who are employees, rather than self employed. However, many suggestions may apply to other groups.

6

YOUR FINANCIAL PLANNING TEAM

Solomon wrote, "Plans fail for lack of counsel, but with many advisors they succeed." That bit of wisdom is particularly appropriate for personal financial planning. No one can single-handedly keep track of all aspects of financial planning. A team effort may be required. Financial planning is an extremely complex field. Depending on your personal goals and financial objectives, you may need advice from several different experts, such as stockbrokers, insurance agents, lawyers, bankers, and accountants. Usually, however, only one person coordinates your financial planning activities. That person is referred to as your personal financial planner.

Traditionally, financial planning advice has been provided by established professionals, such as accountants, insurance agents, and stockbrokers. In addition to these traditional financial advisors, a new category of professionals includes people who specialize strictly in financial planning.

Virtually anyone can claim to be a financial planner. As a result, the financial planning field has its share of frauds and "snake oil" salesmen. State and federal authorities are still in the process of creating methods to certify and regulate planners. Legitimate financial planners and industry groups are very concerned about charlatans in the field. The industry's largest trade group, the International Association of Financial Planners (IAFP), recommends that you have a short meeting with your prospective planner at which time you discuss the following:

1. The planner's background, including education and experience.
2. References, including clients you can call.
3. The planner's competence in different kinds of investments, tax-advantaged vehicles, insurance, and tax strategies. He or she need not be a specialist in all of these areas but should be sufficiently familiar with them to deliver a comprehensive plan.
4. The identity of the person who will actually work with you or supervise and coordinate the efforts of those who will develop the plan. Is it the person you are talking to or a subordinate?
5. The degree of individual attention you will receive. Are all recommendations arrived at independently through a detailed study based on research of your particular situation?
6. The planner's method of compensation. Most professionals base their fees on the complexity of your circumstances and amount of time spent on your affairs. The three basic methods of compensation for financial planners are fee-only, fee and commission, and commission-only.

Certified public accountants (CPAs) constitute one group of traditional financial advisors who are particularly well suited to financial planning. The most prestigious professional accounting society is the American Institute of CPAs (AICPA). All members of the AICPA must be certified public accountants. CPAs are licensed by each state only after they pass a rigorous exam and meet a work-experience requirement.

The AICPA recommends that its members who have a professional interest in personal financial planning join the Personal Financial Planning (PFP) division. Additionally, the AICPA, as part of its Continuing Professional Education division, provides a Certificate of Educational Achievement Program in Personal Financial Planning.

The AICPA also offers a specialty designation, "Personal Financial Specialist" (PFS). To qualify, a CPA, must meet six requirements, including passing a one-day examination, having a minimum of 250 hours of experience in personal financial planning in each of the three years immediately preceding initial application, and providing six references from other professionals and clients.

Exhibit 6.1 provides a list of four prominent financial planning specialist designations and the address of the sponsoring organizations. For more information, you may wish to write these organizations.

While CPAs and other professionals offer high-quality services, they also are relatively expensive. Depending on the complexity of your financial situation, you may either obtain financial planning services from experts or do the planning yourself. Insurance agents and stockbrokers generally offer free financial advice, but you must be cautious when considering their recommendations. Typically, they receive various commissions on their products. Be sure that their recommendations are truly based on your personal goals and not on which products provide the highest commissions.

Whomever you select as your financial planner, be prepared to discuss your personal feelings and concerns without withholding any information. Be as clear as possible regarding your financial goals (see Key 3). You have the right to clear explanations for any recommendations from your financial planner. Ask questions. Don't take any actions without a thorough understanding of the possible consequences.

Financial planning is a team effort that involves you, your personal financial planner, and others. Other team players may include your accountant, your attorney, and your insurance agent. With the appropriate planner, you can move forward to achieve your financial goals.

EXHIBIT 6.1
Financial Planning Specialist Designations

Designation	Sponsoring Organization
CFP- Certified Financial Planner	International Board of Standards and Practices of Certified Financial Planners 5545 DTC DTC Parkway Englewood, CO 80111
ChFC- Chartered Financial Consultant	The American College, Student Services 270 Bryn Mawr Bryn Mawr, PA 19010
RFPP- Registry of Financial Planning Practitioners	The International Association for Financial Planning Two Concourse Parkway, Suite 800 Atlanta, GA 30328
PFS- Personal Financial Specialist	American Institute of Certified Public Accountants 1211 Avenue of the Americas New York, NY 10036

7

CASH MANAGEMENT: BUDGETING

A cash budget is crucial to gaining control of your financial future and ultimately achieving financial success. The motivation for maintaining and sticking to a family cash budget is that it enables you to cover all your bills by paying according to a cash management agenda and to have some money left over for savings and investment. Proper saving and wise investments will enable you to prepare for your future needs.

Cash flow is the term used to describe the flow of money into and from your accounts (that is, cash inflows and outflows). A cash flow statement shows what came in and went out of your bank account during the selected time period. Cash inflows, or sources of cash, include resources such as employment and investment income. Cash outflows, or uses of cash, include purchases of necessities and other items, charitable contributions, and tax payments. Net cash inflow is the excess of total cash inflows over total cash outflows. Net cash outflow means that your total cash outflows exceed total cash inflows.

The first step in cash management is examining your historical expenses. You can start by filling out the worksheet in Exhibit 7.1 with figures from the previous year to produce a cash flow budget for that year.

Next, prepare a projected cash flow budget for the coming year based on your prior year's figures, but make adjustments for any anticipated changes in income and expenses for the coming year. Exhibit 7.2 shows some estimated expenses as a percentage of your net income. These are, of course, only estimates, and depend ultimately on your personal circumstances and tastes.

If last year's cash budget shows a net cash outflow, try to reduce various cash outflow accounts as you prepare your projected cash budget for next year. Exhibit 7.3 suggests ways to cut expenses. Other possibilities include reducing the balance on your credit cards by taking out loans at much lower rates in order to pay them off. After paying off your credit card debt, it is good advice for most people to never again accumulate debt on credit cards. *Always pay off all your credit card purchases each month* so that you don't have to pay any finance or interest charges. Remember that consumer interest is not deductible for tax purposes. But credit cards do give you almost a 30-day float *if* you pay the balance off on time. In essence, the merchant pays for your 30-day float. If you cannot limit your credit card purchases to what you can afford to pay each month with cash, then you probably are better off with no credit cards.

Once your monthly cash inflows exceed your monthly cash outflows, you are on your way to investing for the future. However, before you begin investing, you need an emergency *liquid* fund, or savings cushion (for instance, six months' living expenses) in order to cope with unanticipated future expenses. If last year's cash budget shows a net cash inflow, calculate how long it will take to accumulate your savings cushion. Consider any decreases in expenses that might allow you to achieve your savings cushion faster. Then you need to save an additional six months of expenses in *semiliquid* positions.

Divide the projected annual cash budget by 12 to get the monthly figures for cash inflow and cash outflow. Keep accurate records of cash inflows and cash outflows for the next three months to determine if your monthly cash budget is working. If your budget is not matching up with your actual cash inflows and outflows, then you should consider making appropriate adjustments to your budget.

For financial success, you simply must gain control of your cash inflows and outflows. Financial planning experts can help you determine how to manage your finances, but financial planning experts can never totally replace the need for your personal involvement in the financial planning process. Furthermore, outside experts have less at stake if your financial plans fail. And even if the expert's advice is perfect, ultimately it is up to you to see that those plans are implemented. If your recreation expenses are budgeted at $100 per month, then you must limit your spending to that amount. For a budget to work, you must be disciplined.

EXHIBIT 7.1
Cash Flow Budget

Cash Inflows

Wages or salary	$_____
Spouse's wages or salary	$_____
Interest and dividends	$_____
Rent and royalty income	$_____
Other	$_____
Total Cash Inflows:	$_____

Cash Outflows

Rent or mortgage payments	$_____
Food	$_____
Clothing	$_____
Utilities	$_____
Eating out	$_____
Furniture and appliances	$_____
Recreation	$_____
Gas for car	$_____
Car payments	$_____
Car repairs	$_____
Car insurance	$_____
Doctor bills	$_____

	$ _____
Medicine	$ _____
Interest expense	$ _____
Household repairs	$ _____
Life and disability insurance	$ _____
Education (tuition)	$ _____
Day care	$ _____
Taxes (income, property, etc.)	$ _____
Other	$ _____
Total Cash Outflows:	$ _____
Net Cash Inflow (Outflow)	$ _____

EXHIBIT 7.2
Estimated Expenses as a Percentage of Net Income

Expenses	Single no Children	Single with Children	Married with Children	Married no Children
Housing	20	22	25	23
Loan payments	10	5	5	7
Food	9	12	12	12
Recreation	10	7	5	10
Child care	0	6	5	0
Auto or transit	6	7	7	5
Utilities and phone	5	6	6	5
Clothing	5	4	4	4
Savings	5	5	5	5
Pension	5	5	5	5
Health	3	4	4	5
Education	5	3	3	3
Gifts and contributions	10	10	10	10
Vacation	5	2	2	4
Insurance	1	1	1	1
Other	1	1	1	1

EXHIBIT 7.3
Simple Methods to Cut Expenses

Method	Monthly Saving
Subscribe to newspapers and magazines rather than buying them on newsstands	$10
Buy food in larger quantities	$40
Use newspaper and magazine coupons	$10
When vacationing, stay in less expensive hotels	$20
Increase insurance deductibles	$20
Fill up with self-serve gas	$10
Do your own laundry	$30
Pay off credit cards faster	$20
Prepare your own tax return	$75 to $225 (per year)
Return recyclable bottles	$5
Bring lunch to work	$100
Quit smoking and drinking beer	$100 to $150
Don't buy it just because it's on sale	$5 to $100
Mow your own yard	$20 to $40
Have an interest-bearing checking account	$10 to $30
Learn to do some plumbing and basic household repairs	$30 to $40
Avoid impulse buying	$15 to $30

8

RECONCILING YOUR CHECKBOOK

A checking account is virtually a necessity for managing personal finances. Each check provides a record of purchases and paid bills, and the financial record provided by your checkbook is an invaluable tool for financial planning purposes.

To use your checkbook effectively, you should adhere to the following guidelines:

1. Enter all checks written on and all deposits made to your account immediately. Never postpone recording checks or deposits. Procrastination leads to inaccurate records.

2. Reconcile your bank statement as soon as possible after the statement is received, usually once a month.

3. Always pay your bills at the proper time. If you receive a bill before the due date, you may wish to postpone payment until that time in order to maintain access to your money for as long as possible. On the other hand, if small amounts are involved, it probably isn't worth delaying payment and possibly forgetting to pay on time. *Always pay on time*, especially if there is a discount for timely payment. To ensure that each check is issued on a timely basis, mark the payment due date on your calendar.

4. File all receipts for bills paid by check. The receipt and check may be needed for future use, such as to document a tax deduction. A file system should be

established for storing these records; such a system ensures that you have the necessary information for resolving any discrepancy that might arise regarding a past payment and for preparing your tax returns. The file system also helps you to track your expenditures over time, to make any corrections necessary to your cash budget, and to gain better control over your cash flows.

The bank statement sent to you periodically, usually once a month, shows the *bank's* record of disbursements and receipts concerning your checking account. You should reconcile the statement with your records (your checkbook) in order to verify the accuracy of your records and to discover if any errors have been made by the bank. The bank's record of your checking account and your record of your checking account will differ for two reasons: (1) erroneous entries made either by you or by the bank, and (2) differences in timing when transactions are recorded by you and by the bank. Timing differences may occur, for example, if you write a check and deduct it from your balance but the bank does not process the check and subtract it from your account balance before preparing your statement.

Exhibit 8.1 provides an example of a bank reconciliation. The goal of the bank reconciliation is to find the "true" cash balance in your checking account and to enable you to discover any errors made either by you or by the bank.

Begin with the bank's record of your checking account balance. Add any deposits and subtract any checks written that are recorded in your checkbook but that are not shown on the bank statement. Second, adjust the bank's balance for any errors made by the bank. Bank errors are much less likely than your errors. The resulting number is the true cash balance in your checking account.

To verify the accuracy of the true cash balance based

on the bank balance, you must update your checkbook balance for items recorded by the bank but not recorded by you. Begin with the checking account balance shown in your checkbook. Subtract any bank charges and checks that you deposited that were returned for nonsufficient funds (NSF). If you have an interest-bearing checking account, add any interest earned to your checkbook balance. If there are no errors in your checkbook records, the resulting number also should be your true cash balance and match the earlier calculation. All items that affect "balance per the books" (see Exhibit 8.1) must be recorded in your checkbook register.

Another approach to finding the balance of your checking account is to add to the bank's record of your checking account balance (shown on the bank statement) any deposits made, then subtract any checks you have written that the bank has not yet processed, and that are therefore not on the bank statement. This procedure does not permit you to discover any errors made by the bank and should, therefore, be used in conjunction with a bank reconciliation to find the true cash balance.

EXHIBIT 8.1
Hannah Tracy
Bank Reconciliation, July 31, 2003

Balance per the bank statement, July 31, 2003		$5,000
Add:	Deposit in transit	900
	Bank error, check drawn by Jacob Lawrence	110
	charged to the account of Hannah Tracy.	
Less:	Outstanding checks:	
	Number 96-$35	
	Number 102-$25	
	Number 108-$40	
	Number 110-$20	(120)
"True" cash balance, July 31, 2003		
		$5,890

Balance per the books, July 31, 2003		$5,500
Add:	Note collected by the bank	395
	Error made in recording check #103	55
	Interest earned	15
Less:	Bank charges	(20)
	NSF check	(55)
"True" cash balance, July 31, 2003.		$5,890

9

RECORDKEEPING SUGGESTIONS

Records are necessary for tax and nontax purposes. Adequate records can be simple to maintain:

1. Be sure that your checkbook and check register are accurate and up to date.
2. Use organized files or envelopes for saving receipts and other paper material.
3. Develop a way of summarizing your annual income and expenses; several computer programs are now available for that purpose.

Use checks to pay bills, especially those for tax-deductible items. Your check provides evidence that you paid. On the check, write the purpose of the payment, for example, charitable contribution or federal income tax payment. Be sure to write your Social Security number on any check that is used to pay the U.S. Treasury Department.

In your check register, write the usual information clearly and place a checkmark or other indication in a designated column if your payment is tax deductible. That simple notation will help you to identify quickly deductible items at the end of the year.

Before the start of each year, buy a set of folders, envelopes, or files to help organize all of those loose scraps of paper you will receive during the year. Perhaps 10 folders will be enough, although 30 might be too few for those with many sources of income and expenses. Label each folder with the year and account or purpose, such as Charitable Contributions—2002. Consider using a different color label for each year. Especially at the start of the year, you will have business pertaining to both the current and the previous year. Color coding can prevent misfiling. Be sure to mark each invoice you pay with the date and check number. This process will help you find things when needed. Start a system that you will use.

Summarize the year's financial activity using a pad with columns, a spreadsheet computer program, or a packaged personal financial computer program (see Key 10).

Such a simple system for data retrieval may help you in both tax and nontax disputes, such as obtaining service for an item under warranty and submitting insurance claims. It may also help you in the budgeting and investing processes.

Keep a record of large or unusual transactions even though they have no tax significance. For example, if your Aunt Helen gives you a $500 birthday present, be sure to note the gift in your records. Otherwise, years later when the IRS asserts that the gift is taxable income, you may not remember the source of the money. If you give $2,000 cash to your favorite charity, get a receipt. A canceled check by itself is insufficient. The IRS believes that some seemingly generous donors receive "change" in return for their large contributions. If you give valuable property to a charity, a valuation appraisal will be helpful and perhaps necessary.

Use a contemporaneous diary or log to note car mileage and transportation expenses spent for business, medical, or charitable purposes. Do you entertain clients? If so, a good policy is to pay with a credit card and to write the client's name and the business purpose or discussion on your receipt. An IRS agent also may ask to see your diary or day planner to check the consistency of appointments and deductions. The agent may have noted the date of an ice storm or blizzard that shut down all roads; if your log shows normal travel on that day, it will lose credibility. IRS Publication 552 describes recordkeeping requirements for individuals; Publication 583 outlines these for businesses.

Keep a record folder for documentation of every expenditure that can be added to your home's tax basis, such as hot tubs, mailbox, storm and screen doors, garbage disposals, curtains and draperies. You will need to keep these records until you dispose of your home. The increase in your home's basis may decrease any future taxable gain on the sale of your house.

Accurate records of your stock transactions are important. If you can identify the shares of stock or bonds sold, your basis is the actual cost or other basis of that particular stock or bond. However, if you have purchased securities at various times and cannot identify the shares that are sold, you must follow the first-in, first out rule. In other words, your basis in the securities sold is the basis of the securities acquired first. You may use the average price per share to figure gain or loss on the sale of mutual fund shares.

10

FINANCIAL PLANNING COMPUTER SOFTWARE

Among the most popular of all microcomputer software packages are personal financial planning (PFP) software packages. Many PFP packages are available, offering a wide variety of features and carrying an equally wide variety of price tags. Most, however, cost from less than $50 to about $200. The most basic packages provide a computerized checkbook and maintain your checking account, automatically calculate the checkbook balance, and print checks. More advanced programs provide for budgeting and preparing a net worth report.

Most PFP software packages are written for the IBM PC and PC-compatible computers, although some are also available for the Apple Macintosh (or both PC and Mac). Information on specific software can be obtained from local computer software retailers, computer vendors, software mail-order companies, industry publications, and current users of such software.

Before buying any type of software, you should see a demonstration of the software on a computer system similar to the one you own. If at all possible, talk to people who are currently using the software; ask them about any problems they have encountered.

One typical PFP program is Quicken by Intuit Software Inc. of Palo Alto, California (*www.intuit.com*). Quicken provides for checking, budgeting, general accounting, and single-entry bookkeeping. Support is provided by manual, online, phone, and tutorial. Quicken allows for importing and exporting data from and to spreadsheet software, such as Microsoft Excel, and features a menu-driven system, a help screen, and customization of accounts.

PFP software should be able to perform calculations quickly and should include a reference manual with an index. A program's budget report should show the time period covered, expense accounts with actual and budgeted amounts, and the difference between actual and budgeted amounts. More advanced programs should compute totals for specific accounts, such as checks to the phone company. To use PFP software successfully, you must consistently enter data into the program on a timely basis.

An alternative to using personal financial planning software programs is to design your own financial planning reports using a spreadsheet program. Spreadsheet programs are second only to word processing programs in popularity.

Popular spreadsheet programs include Excel by Microsoft Corporation of Redmond, Washington; and Quattro Pro by Corel Corporation of Toronto, Canada. If you already use a spreadsheet program, then you can easily type in the worksheets described in previous keys, including:

1. Personal Balance Sheet (Key 2)
2. Personal Goals (Key 3)
3. Cash Budget (Key 7)
4. Bank Reconciliation (Key 8)

By typing in your own financial planning reports, you can customize them to your individual needs. For example, you add or delete items to the example of a personal balance sheet previously provided. You may even wish to type your checkbook register into a spreadsheet file to facilitate computing the current balance in your account.

Whether you choose to create your own report forms using a spreadsheet program or use a personal financial planning program, a computerized approach to financial planning offers several advantages to a manual approach.

- Calculations are rapidly and accurately made.
- Reports can be efficiently prepared and printed.
- Updates and changes can be easily made.
- Computerized applications facilitate "what-if" analyses.

Computerized software can help you gain control of your finances by improving recordkeeping and making report preparation (for example, a net worth statement) easier. On the other hand, computer systems, like manual systems, require you to exercise financial discipline. Buying a computer and software won't solve all your financial problems. You still have to stick to your budget, whether it is prepared using pencil and paper or using computer software and printer.

11

FINANCIAL PLANNING RESOURCES ON THE WEB

A number of web sites are available to assist you with financial planning. Exhibit 11.1 lists a dozen useful web sites that can be accessed on the Web (*http://acct.tamu.edu/smith/pfp/*). Each of these is briefly described below.

Bank of America (*http://www.bankofamerica.com/*) is one of the largest financial institutions in America. Its web site provides online banking services, and an entire area of the web site is devoted to personal finance. The personal finance page has links to resources such as mortgage solutions, retirement planning, home equity loans, and credit card debt. Bank of America's web site is massive and has a wealth of information related to financial planning.

Century 21 (*http://www.century21.com*) is one of the country's top real estate corporations. The Century 21 web site is geared toward providing information about purchasing and selling a home. Features of this web site include an online mortgage application, an office locator, and many tips on how to handle the transactions of buying or selling a home.

CNBC (*http://www.cnbc.com*) is a major financial news network on television. Its web site tracks all of the important financial and headline news of the day, and has many user-friendly features. Some of these features are a personalized portfolio tracker, stock quotes, investment research material, and many links to other financial web sites.

E*Trade (*http://www.etrade.com*) is one of the largest online investing services available on the Web. E*Trade's Portfolio Manager lets you create portfolios for all the investments you want to track, whether you hold them at E*Trade or elsewhere. E*Trade offers online investing in stocks, options, bonds, IPOs, and over 5,200 mutual funds. E*Trade provides real-time quotes and customizable charts on thousands of stocks. It also offers banking services. E*Trade was founded as a service bureau in 1982 by Bill Porter, a physicist and inventor with more than a dozen patents to his credit. The early E*Trade provided online quote and trading services to Fidelity, Charles Schwab, and Quick & Reilly. In 1992 E*TRADE Securities, Inc., one of the original all-electronic brokerages, was born and began to offer online investing services through America Online and CompuServe. Following the launch of *www.etrade.com* in 1996, demand for E*Trade's services dramatically increased.

Fannie Mae (*http://www.fanniemae.com/*) provides a steady stream of mortgage funds to America's home buyers by purchasing home loans from a myriad of financial institutions. Its web site is mainly devoted to providing mortgage information and giving links to potential home buyers. Some of the features of the web site are property listings, links to sites where mortgages can be applied for, and information on their mortgage businesses.

Fidelity Investments (*http://www.fidelity.com*) is one of America's premier brokerages. Its web site provides resources for managing a portfolio, online trading, and planning for the future.

Freddie Mac (*http://www.freddiemac.com/*) is very similar to Fannie Mae in its business. Much of its web site is also devoted to giving a great deal of mortgage information. Plenty of resources are available with regard to mortgage planning and obtaining a home loan. Much of this information overlaps with that of Fannie Mae.

HUD (*http://www.hud.gov/*), the U.S. Department of Housing and Development, strives to provide every American with affordable housing. Its web site provides links for buying a HUD home, applying for public housing, and a wealth of information with regard to purchasing or selling a house. The HUD site is very large, with a great deal of information on home ownership in general and many specialized areas as well.

Intuit Corporation's web site (*www.intuit.com*) provides a link to a number of financial calculators (*http://www.intuitadvisor.com/intuit/vortal/gtf/financalc_draw.gtf*). Among the financial calculators provided on the web site are the following:

- home affordability calculator
- investment yield calculator
- mortgage qualification calculator
- savings goal—monthly deposit calculator
- rent versus buy calculator

Morningstar (*http://www.morningstar.com/*) is a financial information service that provides investors with lots of valuable information. Much of the site can be personalized to track your own investment portfolio. In addition, you can sign up for a premium membership to obtain exclusive analyst reports, stock picks, and other resources.

Quicken (*http://www.quicken.com*) provides online and software applications to help people manage their finances. The web site provides investment information, loan information, software support, and tax planning help. Quicken is one of the most trusted names in personal finance management and has an outstanding web site.

Wells Fargo (*http://www.wellsfargo.com*) is a large bank that provides a range of services on its web site. It also has a personal finance section on the web site filled with investment, mortgage, and financial planning pages. Wells Fargo has many features that allow you to personalize them by signing up for an online account.

Yahoo! Finance (*www.finance.yahoo.com*) provides a wealth of investment research material, stock quotes, analyst reports, and other financial information that allows you to manage your own portfolio. In addition it has links to many of the other financial information services and institutions.

In addition to the web sites already described, you can use a Web search engine to look for information on financial planning topics. Search engines provide Internet users a tool for locating and retrieving "data" from the World Wide Web, the major component of the Internet, based upon keywords supplied by the user. All search engines share three basic elements: (1) a "spider" (also referred to as a "crawler" or a "bot") that goes onto the Web and reads pages following hypertext links to other pages and sites on the Web, (2) a "program" that configures the pages that have been read by the spider into an index, and (3) a "second program" that takes user-supplied keywords and "searches" the index, essentially a process of comparison and matching based on the engine's criteria, returning to the user a set of results. The results are usually ranked according to how closely they match the keywords (for instance, home mortgage), defined by the search engine's set of criteria. Each search engine uses a slightly different combination of criteria, with different weights applied. Exhibit 11.2 shows a number of popular search engines that can be accessed on the Web (*http://acct.tamu.edu/smith/search.htm*).

EXHIBIT 11.1
Personal Financial Planning Web Sites

Bank of America	Includes an entire section devoted to personal finance.
Century 21	Valuable information on mortgages and home buying.
CNBC	Official web site of the financial news network.
E*Trade	Online investing service.
Fannie Mae	The federal-backed mortgage corporation provides a large amount of information about obtaining mortgages.
Fidelity Investments	One of the nation's largest investment houses, with a great deal of online resources.
Freddie Mac	Provides a wealth of information about mortgages, and opportunities to purchase a home.
HUD	Links and facts about home buying geared toward the first-time home buyer.
Intuit Corporation	Provides financial planning information and financial calculations.
Morningstar	Investment quotes, information, and research.
Quicken	Provides information devoted to managing personal finances.
Wells Fargo	Information about investments, loans, and mortgages.
Yahoo! Finance	Investment news, research, quotes, and information.

Note: Links to these financial planning web sites are on the Web (*http://acct.tamu.edu/smith/pfp/*).

EXHIBIT 11.2
Web Search Tools

Alta Vista	Subject Directory. Very large database. Search by string of words within text contained in various web sites.
Cyber411	Thorough research. Parallel search engine.
Excite	Advanced search techniques such as word weightings.
HotBot	Very large database. Includes diverse subject directory.
InfoSeek	Very large database. Search FTP, Gopher, and Telnet.
Lycos	Categories. Site reviews. City maps. Stock quotes.
Magellan	Search FTP, Gopher, and Telnet. Site reviews.
MultiCrawl	Parallel Search Engine. A new and highly effective search engine.

Northern Light	Over 150 million web pages and the Special Collection of more than 5,400 full text sources.
Searchopolis	Filtered search engine.
WebCrawler	Backward searches. Many categories.
Yahoo!	Numerous categories. Easy links to info such as city maps and stock quotes.
Yahooligans	Filtered web guide for kids.

Note: Links to these search tools are on the Web
(*http://acct.tamu.edu/smith/search.htm*).

12

MANAGING DEBT: CREDIT

How much debt is acceptable? Many Americans owe more than they own; consequently, they are economic failures. All of them hope to turn their situation around before it's too late, or at least before they have to quit working. Most people want to reach a point in life where they can retire from work and live in relative comfort. To do so, one must begin accumulating wealth rather than debt. Accumulating debt is the opposite of accumulating wealth. Only during high inflation is there potential to have a gain from holding a significant amount of debt. In this case, the gain would depend on the interest rate and whether the assets acquired appreciate in value more than the interest charges.

Is it ever appropriate to borrow money? Yes, but only for a few very specific reasons:

1. You don't have any choice. You need a basic amount of food, clothing, shelter, and medical care. Difficult circumstances, such as a catastrophic illness or a flood, may leave you no choice but to borrow money. Borrowing money for survival is not the same as borrowing money for new clothes, toys, and recreation.

2. You can borrow money at no cost; for example, if you charge purchases on a credit card with a 30-day grace period (effectively borrowing money) and pay off the purchases when you receive your billing statement, you won't incur any finance or interest charges. This process also helps establish your credit history.

3. You wish to leverage your investments (see Key 36). Leveraging, or using other people's money, includes an element of risk. Positive leveraging occurs when you generate a return greater than your cost of borrowing (that is, interest expense). For example, a stockbroker may permit you to borrow up to 50 percent of the acquisition price of a stock or security through a margin account. If the interest charges on the margin account are 10 percent, then you are in a positive leverage position as long as your investment earns more than that. The danger is that your investment may not provide the return you anticipated. Negative leveraging is disastrous and buying stock on margin is not encouraged.
4. You may need to borrow money to acquire an expensive asset, such as a house or car. For many people, saving enough money for these large-dollar items is impossible or impractical. For example, a bank may lend you as much as 90 percent of the cost of a personal residence; consequently, your net equity in your home would be only 10 percent. This is low but still considered acceptable since hopefully the home is not expected to lose more than 10 percent of its value. However, the risk of loss does exist. The housing market can be volatile in certain parts of the country (see Key 21), and prices have fallen by amounts well in excess of 10 percent in some areas.

The best type of loan for you, the borrower, is a "non-recourse" loan, in which the lender has no recourse to the borrower's personal assets for repayment of the loan other than the asset whose acquisition was financed with the debt. A full-recourse loan allows the lender to seek repayment from all the borrower's assets—subject to restrictions imposed by local statutes. Typically, credit card obligations are recourse loans, while secured loans, such as real estate mortgages, could be nonrecourse debt.

Sources of credit include the following:

1. Credit card
2. Personal line of credit at a bank
3. Margin account
4. Whole life insurance policy

Credit cards typically charge the highest interest expense of any source of debt. You should always *avoid deferring payment* on the balance of your credit cards. If you can't do this, you are probably better off without credit cards.

Banks generally offer a personal line of credit to their most creditworthy customers. The interest rate is based on the strength of your personal balance sheet (see Key 2), the relationship you have with the bank, and the amount you want to borrow.

Stockbrokers typically allow you to borrow money using your stocks, bonds, or mutual funds as collateral. The interest rate charged is typically some established percentage above the federal funds rate. Brokers usually require you to maintain $2 of collateral for every $1 you borrow. If the value of your securities falls, then you will be required to provide additional cash or other collateral.

A major source of relatively inexpensive credit is the cash value of whole life insurance policies. If you have a "vintage" policy, you may be able to borrow against the cash value at 6 percent or less; however, policies written in the past ten years may have borrowing rates of 8 percent or higher.

As a rule, home mortgage payments should not exceed 20 to 25 percent of your gross salary. Payments on consumer debt (for example, credit cards) should not exceed 10 to 12 percent of take-home pay. Exceeding these limits puts you in a precarious situation (see Key 21).

Even if you don't currently need to borrow money, there may be a time in the future when you need to do so. It is wise to establish credit by borrowing money and demonstrating a pattern of timely repayment. This process can be done without incurring any interest expense. For example, you can use a gasoline company, department store, or bank credit card (such as, Visa or MasterCard) to make purchases and pay off the full balance each month. Thus, you will avoid any interest charges and establish credit at the same time.

Credit can be useful. If you don't have an established credit history, a bank may be reluctant to lend you money. If you don't have a major credit card, some car rental agencies will not rent you a car. Cashing a check may be difficult without a credit card to prove your identity. Having access to some amount of credit is convenient, but you must use it wisely. Large amounts of debt can destroy you financially. And having no credit history is preferable to having a bad credit history.

During bad times people often consider abandoning their house because the value of the house is lower than the mortgage balance. Think twice before you do such a foolish thing. Foreclosure will blacken your credit record for seven years, and you may have some taxable income.

If you merely mail your keys back to the mortgage holder, you also may lose your credit cards. Many credit card companies take away credit cards when they learn that the holder has been foreclosed upon. If the bank sells the house for less than the outstanding mortgage balance, they can sue you for the deficiency—called a deficiency judgment. Also, any forgiveness of indebtedness by a mortgage holder is considered to be taxable income by the IRS.

If you consider filing for bankruptcy, remember that bankruptcy stays on your credit record for ten years—plus you are required to report it indefinitely any time someone asks (such as banks, credit card companies, employees, car dealerships).

Since credit card companies rarely make significant concessions to a debtor directly, other alternatives may be better. You can find a nonprofit debt counseling company in the phone book under "credit counseling." Some are free and some charge a small fee to consolidate your debt payments into one monthly payment over a longer time period. They may be able to negotiate a lower interest rate, but you do have to pay off everything you owe plus any interest. If you pay, nothing is left on your credit report.

Another alternative is a debt negotiator who may be able to settle your debt for as little as 25 cents on the dollar, with payments over three to five years. They may be able to find a lender who will give you a consolidation loan. The bad news is that you have to make a lump-sum payment, and the settlement is recorded on your credit report for seven years. Since the debt turns from *unsecured* to *secured*, you may lose your home if you do not break your bad spending habits.

13

RISK MANAGEMENT: INSURANCE

Aside from having six months of living expenses in liquid investments (for example, passbook savings account, money market mutual fund, or bank money market deposit account), and six months of semiliquid assets, you should have insurance to shield you from financial disaster. Your safety net of insurance should include health, life, disability, property and casualty, and automobile coverage.

With respect to financial planning, insurance is the item that many people and advisers dislike the most; however, you should protect yourself from loss before you begin to invest for gain. Insurance is an indispensable component in managing your financial affairs.

The amount and type of coverage you need depends upon your obligations to others and the amount of risk you are willing to assume. You need more life insurance when you marry, have children, or incur debt. Your need for life insurance diminishes as you fund your children's education and your net worth increases. A typical person needs from $100,000 to $1 million coverage (around five to ten years worth of income).

There are a variety of life insurance products:

- **Term insurance** provides no-frills insurance protection and does not include a savings element. Term insurance is relatively inexpensive when you are young, but premiums increase with your age. The coverage ends at a foreseeable point, for instance, when mortgage payments end.

- **Permanent insurance** (or cash-value or ordinary life) provides coverage for at least 20 years and insures some long-term need, such as, estate taxes and business needs. The premiums are higher than term insurance in the early years of coverage. These extra premiums go into a fund that builds cash value. Later these earnings can offset insurance premiums. You should buy permanent insurance only if you can maintain the policy for at least 20 years.
- **Whole life insurance** provides protection for an insured's entire life, and the premiums remain the same for the life of the policy. It does include a savings element. Any premiums paid in excess of administrative expenses (commissions, selling, and marketing expenses) and mortality costs are added to accumulated cash values that earn interest. Involves little risk.
- **Variable life insurance** is a permanent insurance contract with level premiums. The cash reserve is maintained in a separate account and the policyholder determines how it is to be invested—equity funds, bond funds, or money market funds. The death benefits vary with the investment return in the separate account, but the death proceeds cannot be less than the policy's original face amount.
- **Universal life insurance** is flexible premium insurance that includes monthly renewable term insurance and an investment component. Administrative expenses are deducted from each premium payment, and any remainder is added to the policy's accumulated cash value. This type of insurance defers current income taxes on policy earnings. If interest rates drop significantly, your premiums will rise.
- **Universal variable life insurance** combines the flexible features of universal life and variable life policies. You may be able to invest in stocks.

- **Single-premium life insurance** involves paying a one-time premium for a specified amount of life insurance protection. Earnings on the investment grow and are tax-deferred as long as they are not withdrawn or borrowed.

You should have health and disability coverage. If your employer-provided health insurance offers insufficient coverage, you should obtain additional major medical coverage independently. Try to get group insurance through some affiliation other than your employer (such as professional societies, labor unions, religious groups, or college alumni associations).

Health maintenance organizations (HMO) are prepaid health care plans that provide medical care, but you must use HMO member doctors and not other doctors, as is possible with a private carrier.

A variation on the HMO concept is a Preferred Provider Organization (PPO). With a PPO, hospitals and doctors agree to provide a company's employees with health services at a discounted rate.

Disability insurance provides income if you become sick or injured and are unable to work. The younger and more active you are, the more coverage needed. A 32-year-old male has a six and one-half times greater risk of being disabled for three months or longer than he does of dying during his working years. Since Social Security disability insurance does not protect all of your income (it pays a maximum of $1,300 a month), you should have enough disability insurance to cover the difference between your monthly expenses and all the income you will receive from other sources if you are disabled.

Avoid a disability insurance policy that contains an "any occupation" clause since benefits stop if you take another job to earn money. The policy should have an "own occupation" clause that allows you to work part time. Make sure the policy is also guaranteed renewable. You can save on your premiums by choosing a policy with a longer waiting period (two or three months) for benefits.

Don't forget property insurance that covers 100 percent of the replacement value of your home and belongings. A replacement cost policy stops the insurer from deducting for depreciation. An "open peril" coverage policy (Form 3 or HO-3) is recommended by many experts. If you are a renter, get an HO-4 policy. An HO-6 policy covers owners of condominiums and cooperatives. Your coverage should include at least 80 percent of the actual cost of rebuilding your home. If you have to file a claim after a fire or theft, you will need valid evidence of what was in your home. Videotape or photograph the contents of your home or have an inventory prepared of your household goods. Store such evidence *outside* of your home (such as in a safe deposit box). This evidence can be used for any casualty loss deduction for tax purposes.

Obviously, you need insurance coverage for your other assets: real estate, automobiles, and boats. A well-designed auto insurance policy is necessary to shield you from a financial disaster. Do not skimp on bodily injury liability coverage. With so many surplus attorneys in most states, lawsuits are common.

Shop around for your insurance and compare the products of different companies. Ask the agent about his or her commissions. An insurance agent is in the business to make money and may sell you the insurance that gives the most commissions and not necessarily the best performance. Consider buying a policy directly from the insurer without sales commissions.

Commissions can be substantial for life insurance policies. Agents' commissions may be 50 to 120 percent of the premiums you pay in the policy's first year. There may be subsequent payments each year of 5 percent or more. A no-commission policy gives you a big head start in accumulating policy value. Bargain well. Agents have considerable flexibility in determining the level of commissions they receive, and they may receive expense allowances and production bonuses from the insurers above their base commissions. You can get a useful sampling of prices and the names of low cost providers on the Web through Insweb (*www.insweb.com*) and Quotesmith.com (*www.quotesmith.com*).

The importance of insurance varies throughout your lifetime. Karen S. Damato, writing for *The Wall Street Journal*, outlines these aspects based upon age:

20s to 30s

- Weigh insurance tab in picking a car.
- Buy renter's policy for an apartment.
- Inventory what you own.
- Look to term life for lowest cost protection.
- Check your disability plan.

40s to 50s

- Consider an "umbrella" policy.
- Check coverage for jewelry, furs, computers.
- Ask about auto policy discounts.
- Review life insurance needs.
- Shop before "converting" term life.

60 plus

- Review homeowner's coverage.
- Weigh long-term care plans.
- Consider trusts for life policies.
- Study ways to tap policy values.
- Get second opinion on buying life insurance for estate needs.

14

LIVING ON ONE INCOME

This key is for the two-income household in which one wage earner loses his or her job or for the two-income family that wishes voluntarily to cut back to one income.

Can two live as cheaply as one? No, but most families that want to live on one income can probably do so. Many people erroneously believe that two incomes are essential to afford the basic needs of a modern family. The fact is that the financial benefits of a second income are often exaggerated. The disadvantages of a two-income family are numerous: day-care concerns, hectic schedules, fast food diets, restaurant meals, and paid housekeepers. If you would like to consider living on one income, then you may benefit from the following strategies:

1. Identify the items on which you spend your money. Make a record of all your purchases for a month or two. Most people are amazed at how the little things add up. If you have an up-to-date budget, then you can skip this step.
2. Identify all the expenses associated with the second job, such as child care, commuting, work clothes, business lunches, and so on. Deduct these expenses from the second job's income. Also, remember to deduct taxes and other withholdings. How much is left? That's the amount by which you have to cut your expenses in order to live on one income. Several areas in which you may be able to save money are described.

- You can help minimize your automobile expenses by keeping your car well maintained. An auto that is properly cared for should last at least ten years. When you have to replace your vehicle, consider buying a used car. Shop very carefully. Search the classified ads. Car dealers typically have a substantial markup above what individual sellers would charge for a similar car. Prior to purchase, be sure to have the car inspected by a dependable mechanic.
- Is it possible for you to cut your clothing costs? The average family of four spends over $2,500 annually on clothes. The key to cutting this amount is to use what you have. Most people have closets full of clothes, but they are unable to resist buying unnecessary additional items. When new clothes are needed, begin your shopping at the lowest-priced stores such as thrift shops, consignment shops, and discount stores. You may also find some things at garage sales.
- The average family of four spends about $800 per month on food. There are several ways this amount can be reduced without sacrificing nutritional quality, variety, or dining pleasure. The first step is to identify the places that provide the most economical prices for basic food items. Check out the warehouse stores and farmers' markets, as well as supermarkets in your locale. Once a month, visit each one to purchase a month's supply of whatever food items that shopping place offers most economically. Shop with coupons.

   The second step is to prepare meals at home. Typically, the cost of home-prepared meals is one-fourth or less of the expense of convenience or prepared foods. If you think your time is too valuable to spend cooking, consider that many simple meals require only ten minutes of hands-on preparation.

The third step is to consider planting a small garden. A garden and a chest freezer can help cut your food bill by several hundred dollars per year. For many people, gardening also serves as an enjoyable and relaxing hobby.

- How much do you spend on toys each year? By age five, the typical child has owned and discarded over 200 toys. Rummage sales, yard sales, and garage sales frequently include toys that look new for a small fraction of their original price.

- Have you purchased any exercise equipment? Do you use it? Millions of people have stored their exercise bikes, step machines, and treadmills in the closet or garage. Likewise, health club memberships typically go unused. Walking and biking are two good examples of cheap but effective exercise. If you want some exercise equipment, check out the garage sales and resale stores.

- Americans spend small fortunes on recreational items and activities, which usually involve sitting, listening, and watching. Entertainment is generally an expensive, indolent activity. Instead of paying to sit through a movie or a sports event, you might visit a free or inexpensive attraction in your area. Go to early movies or rent the movie. Take a Frisbee to the park. Visit a historical site. Go to the lake or beach. You may want to begin a productive hobby such as painting, sewing, woodworking, writing, or baking. Recreation does not have to be passive or unproductive.

3. The biggest expenditure for most people is their house. To become a one-income family, you may consider moving to a smaller house with a lower

mortgage payment. Before buying a house, you should examine as many houses as possible. If you can visit 25 to 50 houses, not only will you be more likely to get a bargain, but you'll be more likely to get the ideal home with the features you want. When financing a home mortgage, you are usually better off with the shortest possible term, such as 15 years, instead of the traditional 30 years.

4. At home, you should minimize your utility bills. Some utility companies offer free energy audits. Air-conditioning and heating bills can be reduced by ensuring that doors and windows are sealed properly. Natural gas is the most economical energy source for heat-generating devices such as stoves, ovens, and hot water heaters. You can reduce your water bill by installing specially designed shower heads and toilets that minimize water use. These items usually pay for themselves in less than a year.

After reading about the steps listed, ask yourself if a second income is really necessary. Do you want to live on one income? If it is financially feasible and you are willing to make the required lifestyle changes, you can do it.

15

RISK AND RETURN

Once you know your goals and objectives, you are ready for saving and investing. Setting aside money on a monthly basis is the best way to accumulate wealth. Saving money should become a habit. When you consider any investment, remember that risk and return are a trade-off. As a rule, higher rewards are earned only by riskier investments.

Risk is directly correlated to the uncertainty of the return you can expect. How well a person predicts the future is an important factor in determining the risk involved. The further in the future a return is expected, the greater the risk involved, since it is hard to predict the future with any degree of certainty. The shorter the time horizon, the less the uncertainty involved, so the risk is lower. The more variable the rate of return, the greater the uncertainty.

Many people are risk-averse, meaning that they do not like to give money away unless there is a good chance they will get more in return. How much risk can you tolerate? The greater the risk involved, the greater the potential compensation, but also the greater the chances of loss. Insured certificates of deposits (CDs) and T-bills are the least risky investments and have low levels of uncertainty. Exploratory drilling for oil and futures contracts are risky investments; they involve a great amount of uncertainty.

Investment risks may be classified as either systematic or unsystematic.

Systematic risk results from sociological, economic, and political factors and includes:

- Market risk—the likelihood that the price of an investment will rise or fall in conjunction with the market as a whole
- Purchasing power risk—the impact deflation or inflation has upon an investment
- Interest-rate risk—the probability that an investment's value will vary in response to a change in the market's interest rate

In general, you cannot avoid systematic risks.

Unsystematic risks can be eliminated by moderate diversification. Holding 20 different stocks has been the general rule for many years, but recent research shows that holding 50 to 100 different stocks is better. Associated with the nature of the business enterprise, unsystematic risks include:

- Business risk—the fact that cash flows might not be adequate to sustain the underlying business enterprise
- Financial risk—the possibility that cash flows may not be sufficient to serve the debt used to finance the business

You can reduce your unsystematic risk by maintaining a well-diversified portfolio. For instance, if your portfolio consists of a company producing bathing suits and a company producing ice cream, you may do well only in the hot seasons. If, however, your portfolio consists of a company producing bathing suits and a company producing winter coats, you should make money regardless of the season.

In general, investments with high risks have a greater potential for earnings. A risk-return seesaw matches potential earnings against potential for loss (see Exhibit 15.1). As the seesaw goes up, one faces an increased potential for return but a decreased safety of principal; for example, U.S. Treasury bills have little systematic (market, interest rate, and purchasing power) risk and little business risk but offer relatively low returns.

The amount of risk you can tolerate and the return you need to achieve depends to a certain extent on your stage in life (see Key 5). Many alternative investments are covered in subsequent keys.

EXHIBIT 15.1
Risk-Return Seesaw

Highest Risk   **Highest Return**

Exploratory Drilling
Production Funds
Commodity Futures
Collectibles
Undeveloped Land
Investment Real Estate
Put and Call Options
Junk Bonds
Oil and Gas Participation
Precious Metals
Common Stocks
Mutual Funds
Corporate Bonds
Variable Life Insurance

Variable Annuities
Municipal Bonds
Government Securities
Nonvariable Annuities
Homes
Money Market Funds
Treasury Bills
Certificates of Deposit
Guaranteed Life Insurance
Series EE and HH Bonds
Savings Accounts
Checking Accounts
Lowest Risk   Cash   **Lowest Return**

16

DEFLATION / INFLATION

Inflation can be defined as an increase in the general level of prices. In other words, inflation causes you to need more dollars to maintain the same standard of living. Inflation has become an expected occurrence in modern America; however, in recent years the United States has experienced relatively low overall rates of inflation.

Inflation does not mean that everything is going up in price. Even during periods of substantial inflation, some products may actually decrease in price. For example, because of improving technology, the cost of computer systems has steadily decreased in recent years.

Deflation is the opposite of inflation and occurs when prices are generally falling. Deflation is rare. Deflation last occurred in the United States during the Great Depression. Before that, deflation took place for about 20 years following the Civil War and in the years immediately following World War I. Since the 1940s, however, prices have constantly increased; only the rate of the increase has varied. The long-term trend is up, up, and away.

How does inflation affect financial planning? Basically, for most goods and services, you should plan to spend more in the future than you do in the present. If you need $50,000 a year today, then you will need twice that amount in 12 years if the inflation rate is 6 percent per year.

The "rule of 72" allows you to estimate quickly the impact of inflation. Divide the inflation rate into 72; the result is the number of years before the value of money is cut in half. For example, if the inflation rate is 10 percent, then your money will have only half its current purchasing power in 7.2 years.

Inflation is measured by various price indexes, including the Consumer Price Index (CPI), the Producer Price Index (PPI), and the GNP Deflator. The CPI is based on the cost of a standard market basket of consumer goods and services (used by the IRS and Social Security Administration), while the PPI, which includes about 3,400 products, is an index of wholesale prices. The GNP Deflator is the price index for the Gross National Product (GNP); as a whole GNP is helpful because it includes prices on all goods and services, not just consumer goods as measured by the CPI.

When inflation begins rising at double- or triple-digit rates of 20, 100, or 200 percent per year, significant economic distortions occur. Typically, most business contracts become indexed to a price index or to the currency of a foreign country.

Inflation is an important consideration when you plan for the future. Some types of investments do better than others when the rate of inflation increases. For example, bank certificate of deposits (CDs) have a locked-in interest rate. If the inflation rate increases, the real return on your CD (allowing for the impact of inflation) diminishes. On the other hand, a real estate investment may fare better during periods of rising rates of inflation. If the inflation rate goes up from 5 percent to 10 percent, you may be able to increase the rent or lease payments required from your tenants. Many mortgage companies offer variable-rate loans in which the mortgage interest rate fluctuates according to an appropriate index.

The smart thing to do is to make at least some investments that perform reasonably well during periods of rising inflation. If your portfolio includes only investments that provide fixed rates of return, then your portfolio's value will be decimated during periods of rising inflation. Traditional hedges against inflation include carefully selected investments in real estate, REITs, stocks, tangible assets, and precious metals, such as platinum, gold, and silver.

17

MANAGING INVESTMENTS

Most experts believe you should have about six months of living expenses in liquid assets. Once this safety net is in place, other investments can be considered.

Taking that first step to purchase investments is the most difficult part of building a good investment portfolio. A critical consideration before deciding if you should manage all or part of your investments is whether you have the time necessary to do so. Managing your own investments requires that you read and analyze daily all information that concerns your investments. Being your own investment manager requires time and a sound basis for your investment decisions.

You must decide how to divide your money among stocks, bonds, real estate, money market funds, and other investment instruments. This process is called *asset allocation*. The amount you decide to put into each type of investment has much to do with individual goals and objectives (see Key 3). Asset allocation can have a major impact on your total portfolio return. It is more critical than specific stock selections. A diversified portfolio is one asset-allocation strategy, and a diversified portfolio enables you to withstand market volatility with less trouble.

A primary consideration in developing your portfolio is your "time horizon." Your time horizon refers to where you are now, where you want to be in the future, and for what reasons you are investing. These considerations are determined by your age, annual income, family makeup, future financial obligations, and need for liquidity. For example, the portfolio allocations of a newly married couple in their twenties with no children, a couple in their early forties with two teenagers soon to be entering college, and a single individual at age 55 should be substantially different because of their different time horizons.

Equity investments (see Key 19) should be spread among the major sectors of the economy. These sectors include the automotive, banking, computer, energy, industrial, pharmaceutical, retail, and utility industries. If you are employed by a firm in one industry, don't be afraid of investing in competitive companies that you know are well managed. Be cautious about investing too much in your employer's stock. If the company in which you work fails, you could lose your job and your investment at the same time.

Since you may lack the time or expertise to manage an investment portfolio, you may wish to consider managed investments. Managed investments include mutual funds, unit investment trusts, real estate investment trusts, and limited partnerships.

- A **mutual fund** is a pool of commingled funds contributed by many investors and managed by a professional fund adviser in exchange for a fee. Mutual funds are available to meet a wide range of investment objectives, and nearly 11,000 funds currently serve the needs of investors. These varied needs are being met by the issuance of funds that specialize in municipal bonds, money markets, growth stocks, small company stocks, gold stocks, foreign stocks, sectors, indexes, and so forth (see Key 20).
- A **unit investment trust** (UIT) is a type of closed-end mutual fund that allows you to lock in high yields. A UIT is established when an investment

company acquires various bonds and then sells units of that portfolio to the general public. UITs may consist of tax-exempt or taxable bonds. The UIT offers a method of locking in current interest rates, as with other fixed-income investments. However, the investment is subject to interest-rate risk and default risk like other fixed-rate investments. Default risk is usually low because of the diversification in the portfolio, but interest-rate risk is ever present. Another problem with UITs is that they are not very liquid. An advantage of UITs is that they offer diversification to a small investor who may be unable to acquire enough individual bonds to be adequately diversified.

- A **real estate investment trust** (REIT) invests in real estate rather than stocks and securities. Although real estate is not very liquid, a real estate investment trust allows your real estate investment to be liquid. Almost like mutual funds, many REITs are traded on one of the major stock exchanges.

    REITs are required by tax laws to distribute at 90 percent of their taxable income as dividends or they lose their tax-advantage status. Thus, they generally pay out higher dividends than most other stocks.

18

FIXED-INCOME INVESTMENTS

A fixed-income investment is one in which you invest an initial amount of money (principal), collect interest on that initial amount, and receive back the initial amount when the security matures. Fixed-income investments are generally low risk, as shown in Exhibit 15.1, the risk-return seesaw, in Key 15, but the return on these investments is also typically rather low. There are two chief dangers associated with fixed-income investments: *interest-rate risk* and *default risk*. The chief danger of interest-rate risk is that interest rates will rise, resulting in a decrease in the value of the investment. Default risk is the danger that the borrower will default either on interest or principal payments.

The most popular of all fixed-income investments is U.S. Treasury obligations. Treasury securities are backed by the full faith and credit of the U.S. government and, therefore, offer the investor both maximum safety of principal and a guaranteed yield. The yield is typically less than that of a corporate bond, but Treasury securities have no default risk. However, they are subject to interest rate risk.

The most popular Treasury securities for individual investors are Treasury bills, Treasury notes, and Treasury bonds. Treasury bills have maturities up to and including one year. Treasury notes mature in one to ten years, while Treasury bonds range in maturity from ten to thirty years.

Treasury bills (T-bills) are most commonly offered by the U.S. Treasury with maturities of three or six months. T-bills are issued every Monday in minimum denominations of $10,000 and in increments of $5,000 above the minimum. Investors bid for them at a discount by offering, for example, $99 for every $100 T-bills. At maturity, the investor will receive $100. Yields are expressed on an annual basis, so that in the case of a three-month T-bill purchased for $99, the yield would be the discount of $1 divided by the price of $99 and multiplied by four, because there are four three-month periods in a year. For this example, the yield would be 4.04 percent. The gain of $1 is interest income and subject to federal income tax, but it is exempt from state and local taxes.

Treasury notes (T-notes) mature in one to ten years. T-notes are issued in $1,000 and $5,000 denominations with a fixed interest rate determined by the coupon rate specified in the note. The interest earned is paid semiannually and is exempt from state and local taxes. T-notes have several characteristics that account for their popularity. One is the low $1,000 minimum. Another advantage is that their longer maturities usually mean a greater return for investors than T-bills can provide.

Treasury bonds (T-bonds) make up the smallest segment of the federal debt. T-bonds mature and repay their face value within a period of ten to thirty years from the date of issue. These bonds are issued in denominations of $1,000, $5,000, $10,000, $50,000, $100,000, and $1 million. A fixed rate of interest is paid semiannually, and the interest earned is exempt from state and local taxes. Some T-bonds are callable, or redeemable, prior to maturity. A callable bond is indicated in the newspaper by a hyphen between the call date and the maturity date. For example, if 2001–2005 is listed under "maturity," that means the bond can be redeemed at any time starting in 2001.

U.S. savings bonds are another popular fixed-income

investment. Savings bonds are sold at a discount from their face value. They are highly liquid investments, although if they are cashed in before maturity there is a reduction in the rate of interest earned. Interest from Series EE bonds offers the tax advantage of being exempt from federal income tax until they are cashed in or until maturity.

Corporate bonds are another form of fixed-income investment. Compared to government-backed securities, they carry a greater element of risk. The level of risk depends chiefly on the quality of the corporation issuing the bonds. Consequently, there is great diversity in risk level.

Municipal bonds are issued by state and local governments and offer relatively low risk. Also, they feature significant tax advantages, since they are exempt from federal income tax. There are five major ways of buying into the $1.3 trillion municipal bond market: individual bonds, open-end mutual funds, closed-end funds, unit investment trusts, and single-state funds. If you live in a state with high income taxes, consider the single-state funds because bonds purchased by residents of the issuing state are generally exempt from state and local taxes as well as federal tax.

Other fixed-income investments are customer accounts provided by banks and savings and loan institutions. From lowest to highest level of return, the three most popular types of customer accounts are savings accounts, money market accounts, and certificates of deposit (CDs). Risk is extremely low, and liquidity is high. Consequently, return is relatively low for each of these types of accounts. The federal government, through the Federal Deposit Insurance Corporation (FDIC) for banks and Federal Savings and Loan Insurance Corporation (FSLIC) for savings and loan institutions, offers insurance on customer accounts up to $100,000.

Fixed-income securities also are offered by government agencies other than the Treasury Department. These specialized agency securities are not necessarily as safe as Treasury issues and consequently may carry higher interest rates.

Insurance companies issue another kind of fixed-income investment called an *annuity*. An annuity is sold by the insurance company to an investor, who is guaranteed a fixed return for a certain period of time (such as 10 years, 20 years, or the life of the investor). See Key 36.

For more information see Barron's *Keys to Investing in Government Securities* by Jay Goldinger and *Keys to Investing in Corporate Bonds* by Nick Apostolou.

19

EQUITY INVESTMENTS

Equity investments include investments in corporate stocks. Such stock, in companies publicly traded on the New York Stock Exchange, the American Stock Exchange, and the NASDAQ, is highly liquid. *The Wall Street Journal* is the best-known source of information on daily stock prices, although most major newspapers also publish closing prices, and net change from the previous closing price for individual stocks. *The Wall Street Journal* and *The New York Times* stock market listings also provide the highest and lowest price of each stock during the past 52 weeks, the dividend amount (with corresponding yield percentage), and volume of shares traded.

Stock quotes can also be obtained through the Internet. Many web sites that allow you to maintain a personalized page will also allow you to track a personalized portfolio of stocks on your page. For example, Yahoo! will allow quotes to be maintained for several stocks and for several indexes of your choosing on a "My Yahoo!" page along with other personalized news and services. Stock price services such as these are usually delayed from 15 minutes to an hour and are provided by various news sources. Many sites will also allow you to review historical charts and graphs of these stocks. A brief search of finance sites on the Internet will allow you to locate other services such as real-time quotes that display on the bottom of your computer screen.

Stock market investments range from very high risk to very low risk. Some stocks provide relatively high dividend yields (dividend amount divided by market price of the stock), while others provide no dividends. Growth stocks are those that provide low, if any, dividends, but do offer long-term capital appreciation. In other words, the price of the stock is expected to increase over time. Wal-Mart has been an example of a growth stock.

Income stocks are those that offer little opportunity for capital appreciation but provide relatively high dividends. Most utility companies, such as Philadelphia Electric or Texas Utilities, are considered income stocks. Many companies provide some dividends and are considered combination growth and income stocks. Stocks of automobile manufacturing companies, for example, provide both substantial dividends and opportunities for capital appreciation. A company's board of directors typically sets the dividend policy based on the desires of the management, the stockholders, and applicable laws and regulations.

Value investing involves those stodgy old utilities and industrials such as Allstate, John Deere, Alcoa, Duke Power, Phillip Morris, and Caterpillar. About 200 value-oriented funds disappeared during the Internet boom, when technology stocks were very popular. In the aftermath of the technology stock bust, value stocks regained some popularity.

Fundamental analysis is the process of estimating a stock's value by analyzing the basic financial and economic facts about a company (for example, financial statements). Technical analysis (or charting) attempts to predict future stock price movement by analyzing the past sequence of the stock's prices.

The primary objective of a corporation is to maximize the wealth of its stockholders. This objective can be achieved through the payment of dividends or capital appreciation. In recent years companies have been reducing or omitting dividend payments. By not paying dividends, management can reinvest earnings into the firm's operations. Additional plant and equipment can be purchased, more employees can be hired, and so on. This growth in company assets should lead to higher stock prices. Some experts argue that companies should buy back their stock shares rather than pay or raise dividends.

Dividends do matter because you get paid while you wait. Not until 1958 did the average dividend yield on common stocks in the Standard & Poors 500 Index fall below the yield of long-term U.S. Treasury bonds. Using the argument that dividends are taxable as ordinary income, the tendency to pay dividends has been on the wane. In a book entitled *Dividends Don't Lie,* Geraldine Weiss and Janet Lowe argue that value in blue-chip stocks is well defined and reflected by growth in dividends.

Donald Cassidy, a senior research analysist with a leading financial investment services company and author, states that dividends do matter very much as indicators of corporate health. His research shows a bias toward better stock performance among rising-dividend payers, rather than among static payers or dividend decreasers. Tax-wise, you may wish to put your dividend paying stocks inside a tax-free account (such as Keogh, IRA, 401(k) or Roth IRA, see Key 25). Then put your growth-type shares in taxable accounts. Industries paying relatively high dividends include utilities, REITs, banks, major energy companies, consumer-product companies, and pharmaceutical companies.

The firm's total assets are only one factor that has an impact on the firm's stock price. Even more significant is the firm's expected future earnings. Having a lot of assets does not necessarily ensure high earnings. Automobile manufacturers have tremendous investments in plant and equipment, but if future auto sales are expected to decline, then auto company stock prices will probably decline.

Determining which stocks to purchase is probably

your biggest concern. But first you must determine how much of your total savings and investments should be in stocks. For most people, how much they invest depends on how risk-averse they are. If you dislike any risk, then stocks should constitute a smaller proportion of your total savings and investments than lower-risk investments such as Treasury securities or bank CDs (where a fixed return is virtually assured). Along with the potential of higher returns, stocks bring a corresponding higher level of risk.

Stocks continually rise and fall in price. If it bothers you that your investment constantly fluctuates in value, then the stock market is not for you. Sometimes stock prices fall dramatically, as happened in the stock market crash of October 1987, when the market dropped 508 points, or 26 percent, in one day. In the following years, however, stock prices increased dramatically, greatly offsetting the 1987 downturn. They then plunged in late summer of 1990 as a result of the invasion of Kuwait and the sharp increase in oil prices. In 1994 the market set new highs. NASDAQ first closed over 2,000 on July 16, 1998. In March 2000 NASDAQ went above 5,000 when the tech bubble reached its zenith; but one year later it was down to the 1,600 level. In the 13 months between March 10, 2000 and April 4, 2001 the average tech fund dropped 70.1 percent. The market had a significant drop after the September 11, 2001 terrorist attack.

Over the past 65 years, common stocks have returned an average of 12 percent annually. One of the keys to successfully investing in stock is to maintain a balanced portfolio of stocks. Stocks themselves should be only one component in your total portfolio of savings and investments. Let us assume that stocks represent 50 percent of all of your savings and investments. The other 50 percent of your total portfolio may consist of Treasury securities, bank CDs, and real estate. The 50 percent invested in stock should be allocated among different types of stock, possibly three or more different types of mutual funds. For example, you might allocate one third of your stock holdings to "blue-chip" companies such as Coca-Cola and Procter & Gamble. These companies provide relatively low dividends and are considered growth stocks. These are very safe investments and over the long run should provide a reasonable return. Because they carry some risk, the expected return is greater than the return on a bank CD.

You might allocate the second third of your stock holdings to income stocks, such as utility companies. The final third of your stock holdings could be invested in more speculative companies (see Key 20 about mutual funds).

Before you start investing, you should select one brokerage firm and keep all of your stocks and bonds with that one firm. You can build a better working relationship by using only one broker; furthermore, record-keeping will be simpler. Of course, if you become dissatisfied with your broker's services, you should then switch to another company. Your broker should be the custodian of your investments, a service offered by full-service, discount brokers, and online brokers. The custodial service saves you the unnecessary hassle of dealing with all the paperwork and gives you more time for important decisions. Check out bad brokers at *www.nasdr.com* and *www.nasdadr.com*.

Discount brokers charge lower commissions than full-service brokers, and online brokers charge even less. If you trade online you may wish to have two online brokers in case one is down. One of the largest online brokers is E*Trade (see Key 11). Also, more than 900 companies offer dividend reinvestment plans in which their stock is sold directly to the public, providing savings on commissions. Direct stock purchases, however, require more time, and you must own at least one full share of stock before you can participate in most of these programs.

The best approach to acquiring a balanced portfolio is to invest in a mutual fund, especially an index fund. Instead of acquiring individual shares of stock, you may purchase shares of a mutual fund, which itself is comprised of shares of many different companies (see Key 20). There are about 11,000 mutual funds—more than there are stocks on the New York Stock Exchange.

Some basic investment guidelines are as follows:

1. Determine your investment goals and your risk-tolerance level.
2. Set your target-level annual return for the next three years.
3. Decide how much you can afford to invest each year.
4. Keep track of your investment performance.

Dollar cost averaging. One final consideration in making equity investments is your purchasing strategy. A popular approach is called *dollar cost averaging*. This method seems to work well and is extremely simple. You ignore price trends and invest a fixed amount at regular intervals. Thus, fewer shares will be acquired at relatively high prices and more shares at low prices. This method is especially recommended for purchasing shares in a mutual fund. Choosing to reinvest your dividends is a form of dollar cost averaging.

Some mutual funds offer options to assist with dollar cost averaging. These funds will allow you to make monthly drafts out of your checking account or out of your paycheck to your mutual fund account. This allows the investor to buy shares regularly and may make it easier to consistently invest. Information about these types of purchasing options can usually be found on the mutual fund web site or in the fund prospectus.

Market timing approach. The opposite of the dollar cost averaging approach is the *market timing approach*. In market timing, you attempt to purchase shares when their price is low and to sell when their price is high. Many investment firms offer market timing services. Some are much more successful than others. If you use a market timing service, be sure to investigate the past performance of the service.

Exchange traded funds. Exchange traded funds (ETFs) are the newest kid on the block. ETFs are like an index mutual fund traded throughout the day. A standard mutual fund is priced only at the end of the day. ETFs tend to be cheaper and more tax-efficient than index funds. For example, the so-called "Spiders" or SPDRs have an expense ratio of around 0.17 percent a year, but you do have to pay brokerage fees when you buy and sell them. These spiders give investors an ownership interest in a particular sector or group (such as XLE, energy sector). SPY allows you to index the S&P 500. DIA (Diamonds) allows you to index the Dow Jones average. The Spider MDY allows you to index the S&P 400, and QQQ allows you to index the NASDAQ-100. You can use these exchange traded funds for broad bets on the direction of the markets (see Key 38 for more about iShares).

For more information see Barron's *Keys to Investing in Common Stocks* by Nick and Barbara Apostolou and *Keys to Understanding Securities* by Anita Jones Lee.

20

MUTUAL FUNDS

For individuals who lack the time or expertise to manage an investment portfolio, an excellent investment alternative is to purchase shares in mutual funds. A mutual fund is a pool of the comingled contributions of many investors and managed by a professional fund adviser in exchange for a fee. Mutual funds are available to meet a wide range of investment objectives, with about 11,000 funds currently serving the needs of investors. These varied needs are being met by the issuance of funds that specialize in municipal bonds, money markets, growth stocks, small company stocks, gold stocks, foreign stocks, and so forth.

Two basic types of funds exist: *closed-end mutual funds* and *open-end mutual funds*.

A closed-end mutual fund is an investment company with a fixed number of shares that trade on an exchange or over-the-counter. Most of these stock funds trade for less than their net asset value (at a discount).

Open-end mutual funds, by far the most popular type of mutual fund, are funds that issue or redeem shares at the net asset value of the portfolio. Unlike the closed-end funds, the number of shares is not fixed but increases as investors purchase more shares. These shares are not traded on any market. Typically, large mutual fund organizations manage families of funds that may include, for example, one or more growth stock funds, gold funds, money market funds, bond funds, and small company stock funds. Usually an investor may switch from one fund to another within the same family of funds at no cost or for a small fee. Switching can be done by telephone.

Open-end mutual funds can also be divided into load and no-load funds based upon whether they charge a sales fee when the fund is initially issued. A load fund is often sold by a stockbroker or financial adviser who charges a fee of up to 8.5 percent of net asset value, which is deducted from the amount of the investment.

No-load funds are typically purchased directly from the fund without stockbroker involvement. There is no initial sales charge. Studies have found no evidence that load funds perform better than no-load funds. Even though a fund is no-load, however, fees can lurk in many places. Besides the commission or sales charge (1 to 8 percent), there may be a 12b-1 fee. An SEC rule allows a fund to charge a fee for marketing and distribution that is deducted from the assets of the fund each year (.25 to 1.25 percent).

There are also exit fees or back-end charges for selling your shares. In addition, management fees may be deducted from the fund's assets (.25 to 2 percent).

There are two distinct styles of management in mutual funds: *value* and *growth*.

A value mutual fund emphasizes stocks with above-average dividends. A value mutual fund would be suitable for an individual who is taking distributions from a retirement plan and needs current dividend income for living expenses. Also, a value fund is suitable for an individual approaching retirement who needs a conservative investment, or for someone holding equity investments in a tax-deferred plan where dividends escape current taxation.

Growth mutual funds seek the capital growth potential of firms with above-average earnings growth rates. These funds appeal to individuals who are accumulating assets and to people in high tax brackets hoping to avoid taxes on dividends and experience lower taxes on long-term capital gain. Growth funds emphasize capital growth over income and may have larger share price fluctuations.

Barry L. Cliff, president of American Financial Consultants in Silver Spring, Maryland, suggests asking yourself these ten questions:

1. Do your investment objectives match those of the fund?
2. Can the fund borrow money to invest (leverage), and are you comfortable with the added risk?
3. Is the fund's track record attributable to its current portfolio manager?
4. How well did the fund do in the last "bear" market (2000–2001)?
5. How do the fund's expenses and management fees compare with other funds of comparable size?
6. Does the fund have a 12b-1 fee?
7. Is there a redemption charge or fee if the fund is liquidated at any time?
8. Do you have the flexibility of switching to different funds if your investment objectives change without incurring more than a nominal charge?
9. Can the switch described in number 8 be done by telephone?
10. Are you willing to take the risk of investing in any type of mutual fund?

Since mutual funds diversify your assets, consider investing in four to seven mutual funds, then you have a truly diversified portfolio. But always read the prospectus carefully.

Mutual fund prices are reported daily in the financial pages of newspapers. Funds are listed under the name of the sponsor, such as AAL Mutual Funds (see Exhibit 20.1). The first two columns give the name and abbreviation of the fund, and the third column gives the latest net asset value (NAV). The fourth column provides the last offering price, which includes the maximum sales charge. If there is no sales charge, the column will indicate N.L., meaning no-load. The fifth column indicates the change in the NAV for the previous day.

Before purchasing a mutual fund, an investor should check its performance record. *Barron's Magazine* publishes special mutual fund surveys quarterly in mid-February, May, August, and November, including articles and performance statistics. *Forbes Magazine's* highly regarded survey is published in August or September and features ten-year performance records of all funds, a selective "honor roll" of outstanding funds, and a ranking of how funds have performed in rising and in falling markets. In February of each year, *Business Week* publishes ratings of mutual funds that weigh five years of total returns against the risks taken to make those returns. *Money* publishes regular articles about mutual funds and extensive quarterly statistics on performance. Many of these ratings can be found on the web sites of these magazines, including real-time quotes and search engines to help find funds to meet your goals.

The best-known source of mutual fund information is probably Morningstar. Morningstar offers a mutual fund rating on a monthly basis. These ratings can be found on the Morningstar web site (*morningstar.com*), although many fund information sheets and web sites also offer this information. If you are going to use this to compare funds, be sure that you understand what this information means. The rating is made up of a risk portion and a return portion. After the risk and return scores are calculated on a relative basis for each fund grouping (domestic, international, taxable bonds, municipal bonds), the funds in the group are ranked. Funds with scores in the top 10 percent earn 5 stars; the next 22.5 percent, 4 stars; the middle 35 percent, 3 stars; the next 22.5 percent, 2 stars; and the bottom 10 percent, 1 star. In addition to this information, Morningstar offers other helpful advice about choosing mutual funds, comparing mutual funds, and financial news. Getting the information online requires registration on their web site; however a basic registration is free.

One major problem with mutual funds is taxes, which may reduce a fund's return by 2 to 3 percent. Even if the mutual fund loses money, you still may have to pay a capital gains tax. One alternative for avoiding taxes on mutual funds is to invest in tax-free bond funds, also known as municipal bond funds. These funds usually offer a lower rate of return but are not taxable on your federal income tax return. Analysis will need to be done before investing in these funds to see if the lower returns will be advantageous given your current tax rate. For individuals with lower tax rates, these types of funds may not make economic sense. They may be a nice alternative, however, for those who need to reduce taxable income.

An alternative to a mutual fund is a portfolio on FOLIOfn (*http://www.foliofn.com/joa*). Here you can buy portfolios of one to 50 stocks in one simple transaction. You can trade whole folios or stocks in your folios twice a day. You pay a flat fee each month, and you can invest in "ready-to-go portfolios."

For more information see Barron's *Keys to Investing in Mutual Funds* by Warren Boroson.

EXHIBIT 20.1
Mutual Fund Price Quotations

	Inv.Obj.	NAV	Offer Price	NAV Chg.	YTD	Total Return 39 wks	5yrsR
AAL Mutual:							
Bond p	BND	10.59	11.12	−0.02	+8.6	+6.7	+10.1 C
CaGr p	GRO	15.00	15.75	−0.16	+3.7	+5.2	+13.4 C
MuBd p	GLM	11.23	11.79	−0.03	+9.2	+8.1	+8.8 D
SmCoStk p	SML	10.31	10.82	−0.27	NS	NS	NS

21

REAL ESTATE
INVESTMENTS
(YOUR HOME)

Home ownership remains the great American dream. Thanks to mortgage loans, the dream has become a reality for many Americans. A mortgage loan supplies the cash many people need to purchase a home. The loan is usually repaid over a long period of time, usually 15 or 30 years. Mortgage is defined as a claim on property, given to a person who has loaned money in case the money is not repaid when due. A loan allows you to leverage (see Key 36).

The term *mortgage* has historically carried an implication of servitude. It is derived from an old French word meaning "death pledge," or pledge payable on death. The term *amortize* is also derived from an old French word, which meant "to deaden." The idea of amortizing a loan over a long time period is to deaden the pain of the debt.

Mortgage lenders have an important responsibility to ensure that borrowers can afford their "American dream." Not only does this benefit the borrower, but it also ensures the lender a profitable repayment of the loan. Consequently, all parties to a mortgage loan benefit.

Is a home a good investment? Home prices increased at a double-digit pace during the 1970s. During the 1980s home prices fell in such areas as Texas, Louisiana, California, and Oklahoma. In recent years, home prices have increased only moderately (4 to 5 percent nation-

82

wide) and are expected to exceed the inflation rate only slightly. However, there are still advantages to purchasing a home with a real estate loan.

Paying off a real estate loan (mortgage) builds equity that can sometimes be used as collateral for financing other purchases. Home mortgage interest and property tax are two of the tax breaks remaining in U.S. tax laws. Homeowners can still deduct mortgage interest and property tax from other taxable income. These deductions generated lower tax savings than formerly for many people because of the reduction in individual federal income tax rates in 1986. However, in 1993 the maximum individual rate was raised to 39.6 percent, making home mortgages more attractive as tax shelters. In 2002 and 2003 the highest rate is 38.6 percent.

As a result of the relatively low house price appreciation rates in the mid- and late-1980s, mortgage lenders and insurers generally tightened standards for home loan approvals and minimum down payment requirements. For example, the requirements regarding ratio of size of loan to size of down payment and acceptable level of existing installment debt for the borrower are now more strict. The secondary market for mortgage loans, including the Federal National Mortgage Association, also has mandated stricter requirements than those that existed in the past. Consequently, even though mortgage interest rates in 2001 were substantially lower than in past years, many borrowers found that they qualified for smaller mortgages than they would have in the past.

Stricter lending requirements are designed to protect the lender from bad loans. In the past, the lender could recover from a default because of the appreciation on the property. Because of the low appreciation rates, this cushion no longer exists.

Basic approaches for purchasing a home are not as simple as they used to be. Once, the rule of thumb was to pay roughly twice one's annual salary for a house. Following the inflationary boom of the 1970s, permissible home mortgages grew to a range of 2.25 to 3.24 times the buyer's gross income.

Given current market conditions, you should consider a home as a living expense and not as an investment. Financial instruments generally make better investments than property during periods of low inflation. Financial planners recommend paying off mortgage debt as quickly as possible when the home value appreciation rate is low. Why? The only way to build equity when the home is not appreciating is to reduce the debt on the house. Consequently, the 15-year mortgage is widely used because it builds equity about seven times faster than the traditional 30-year mortgage.

How much can you afford to pay for a home? Most lenders have general rules regarding the maximum loan amount. The National Association of Realtors uses the following method:

1. Calculate the borrower's gross monthly income. To do this, divide the borrower's yearly salary before any deductions by 12. If the borrower's spouse works, do the same for that salary.
2. Deduct monthly payments on long-term debts (such as car loans) from the gross monthly income.
3. Multiply that figure (gross monthly income less long-term debt payments) by .32. The resulting amount is the monthly payment that you can afford, according to most lending guidelines, with a down payment of 10 percent or more.
4. Determine the average real estate tax in the area. Real estate taxes vary substantially from several hundred to several thousand dollars annually. Add 2 to 4 percent for annual insurance premiums, which also may vary substantially. Divide the total by 12 to calculate monthly costs for taxes and insurance. The average monthly cost for taxes and insurance on a $100,000 home would be about $200.

5. Subtract the monthly cost of taxes and insurance from the monthly payment computed in step 3. The resulting figure is how much you can afford to pay for a mortgage each month.

Assume that Willie and Myrtle Barfoot have a combined gross income of $48,000 per year, a monthly car payment of $280, and savings of $20,000. The Barfoots' gross monthly income is $4,000; subtracting the $280 car payment leaves $3,720. Multiplying that by .32 reveals that the family can afford $1,190.40 in monthly payments. After subtracting estimated taxes and insurance costs of $200, a total of $990.40 is left for a mortgage principal and interest payment.

A 30-year, 10 percent, fixed-rate mortgage on $110,000 yields mortgage principal and interest payments of $972.39; thus, that amount is the maximum the Barfoots could pay in today's market based on a conventional fixed-rate loan.

Closing costs average about 4 percent of the mortgage amount on a new mortgage with two discount points. Discount points are finance charges that are calculated by the lender at closing. Each point equals 1 percent of the loan amount. For example, 2 points on a $110,000 loan equals $2,200. Typically, points paid are inversely related to the interest rate charged on the loan. Consequently, the Barfoots must set aside $4,400 of their $20,000 savings, leaving $15,600 for a down payment. They can thus afford to purchase a $125,000 house, putting $15,000 down (a little more than 12 percent), and have enough income to qualify for a mortgage on the remaining $110,000 cost of the house. A number of realty, bank, and title company web pages offer mortgage calculators to give you a quick idea of what monthly payments may be on a certain home given the down payment and total cost of the house. Keep in mind that these calculators are helpful, but will not consider all of the costs that come with home ownership and may not reflect the interest rate that you will actually obtain from your lender.

By plugging your financial characteristics into this formula, you can determine how much home you can theoretically afford. Depending on other financial factors and objectives, however, this amount may be too much for you to spend comfortably on your home. If you are a first-time home buyer or if you have had credit problems in the past, you may still qualify for an FHA loan. These loans can be advantageous to home buyers because they require a smaller down payment of only 3 percent instead of the 5–20 percent required by a conventional loan. In addition, insurance and closing costs may be financed in the mortgage. More information can be obtained about FHA loans online at *www.hud. gov/qualify.cfm* or by contacting the U.S. Department of Housing and Urban Development (HUD).

Bear in mind that there are other considerations in purchasing a home. Property insurance will need to be obtained, and the difference in homeowner's insurance and renter's insurance may be substantial. If a down payment is made that is less than 20 percent of the price of the home, mortgage insurance will also have to be purchased. There are also regular maintenance costs and depending on the size of your new home, utilities may increase. Homeowner's association fees and property taxes should also be considered when determining the cost of home ownership.

If you already own a home, consider refinancing the mortgage with a new loan whenever the interest rates decline. Refinancing does cost money, so you must decide whether the future cost savings justify the costs of refinancing. How much longer you plan to keep the home is important to determine if you should refinance. A simple way is to divide the costs of refinancing by the monthly savings. This calculation, called the *payback method*, will give you the total number of months to recover your investment.

Purchasing a home for the first time can be frustrating and confusing. There are a few things that may make the process easier:

1. Ensure that you are comfortable with the stages of the home-buying process and the vocabulary used in this process. Reading other books, attending home-buying seminars, or reviewing information published by the HUD are all good sources of information. Familiarize yourself with these things prior to beginning the search for a home. This will allow you to feel more confident about your decisions and ensure that you can understand and appropriately evaluate all the information that your real estate professional and lender give you.

2. Find out if your state requires that an attorney be involved in the process. In many states this is not required if a qualified real estate professional is used. Better to know the requirements at the beginning of the process than to try to find an attorney immediately before closing. Also, begin shopping around for a lender and for homeowners insurance. Pre-approval of the loan may speed up the process and may help narrow the search. Also, proof of homeowner's insurance will need to be evidenced at closing, so get your insurer involved up front and shop for the policy that provides you with the best value.

3. Once you have decided to make an offer on a home, you will need to provide earnest money as evidence of your intentions. This money is a percentage of the cost of the home (ranging from about 1–5 percent usually). If your offer is rejected the money is returned to you; if it is accepted, the money is used as part of the down payment or closing costs. If, however, you decide not to purchase the home, this money may be forfeited. Be sure to find out before giving the earnest money in

which cases you will lose the full amount if you do not go through with the purchase.

Other costs that might be involved include home inspections and realtor fees. Realtor fees come out of the price paid for the home and reduce the amount that is received by the seller of the home. Home inspection fees may be the responsibility of the buyer or the seller. In some cases, if the home recently had an offer that fell though, the previous inspection report may be used. It is a good idea to ask if there is a recent report available in order to reduce costs. Some items noted by the inspector may affect the value loaned for your new home and could affect your decision to go through with the purchase. This would include things such as finding termite infestations or foundation problems.

For more information see Barron's *Keys to Buying and Owning a Home* by Jack P. Friedman, *Keys to Mortgage Financing and Refinancing* by Jack C. Harris and Jack P. Friedman, and *Keys to Purchasing a Condo or Co-op* by Jack C. Harris and Jack P. Friedman.

22

HARD ASSET INVESTMENTS

Some of your investments might be in hard assets. Some planners suggest that investors put up to 10 percent of their portfolio into an inflation hedge. *Hard assets* refers to tangibles such as gold and silver, gems, rare coins, stamps, artwork, antiques, baseball cards, antique cars, comic books, and oil and gas.

The following chart should help you in considering an investment in hard assets:

	Volatile	Liquidity	High Mark-up	Reproductions	Altered	Portable	Inflation-hedge	Grading Problems	Dividends Interest
Gold	Yes	Yes	No	No	No	Yes	Yes	No	No
Silver	Yes	Yes	No	No	No	Yes	Yes	No	No
Diamonds	Some	No	Yes	Yes	No	Yes	Yes	Yes	No
Colored Stones	Some	No	Yes	Yes	Yes	Yes	Yes	Yes	No
Art	Some	No	Yes	Yes	Yes	Yes	Yes	Yes	No
Rare Coins	Some	No	Yes	Yes	Yes	Yes	Yes	Yes	No
Stamps	Some	No	Yes	Yes	Yes	Yes	Yes	Yes	No
Antiques	Some	No	Yes	Yes	Yes	No	Yes	Yes	No
Baseball Cards	Some	No	Yes	No	Yes	Yes	Yes	Yes	No
Autos	Some	No	Yes	No	Yes	No	Yes	Some	No
Oil/Gas	Some	No	No	No	No	No	Yes	No	No
Comic Books	Some	No	Yes	No	Yes	Yes	Yes	Yes	No

Gold and silver have historically been a hedge against inflation. The most common ways to buy gold or silver are bullion and coins. Gold and silver also are sold on the commodity exchange. A low-cost way to buy such a metal is to purchase a 1,000-ounce silver bar on the commodity exchange and "take possession." In other words, you pay the full price, and the silver bar is stored in a bank in Chicago. You pay a small storage charge each year.

You may buy gold and silver coins from a dealer for 3 to 5 percent above the daily spot market price. Popular gold coins include the United States gold eagle, the Canadian maple leaf, the South African kruggerand, the Mexican peso, and the Chinese panda.

Hard assets sometimes increase in value even when the value of other investments is declining. For example, one month after the world stock market crash of October 19, 1987, Sotheby's of New York sold *Irises*, a painting by Vincent van Gogh, for $53.9 million. In 1990 van Gogh's melancholy portrait of his physician, Dr. Gachet, sold for $82.5 million. But the art-auction frenzy of the late 1980s has begun to decline, and the contemporary art market began a slide in the early 1990s and was in the doldrums until around 1998. A tiny 16 × 13-inch *Portrait of the Artist without His Beard* by van Gogh sold for $71 million in November, 1998.

A study by L. Renneboog and T. van Houte of 10,500 art sales prices from all over the world (from 1970 to 1997) found that art investments underperform equity market investments due to high riskiness, transaction costs, and insurance premiums. You have limited ways to diversify with art, and collectible capital gains are taxable.

Coin collecting and investing have greatly increased during the past several decades. Those collectors driven by investment goals have become more numerous than ever before. No longer is coin collecting considered to be a hobby only for young boys. More uniform grading has allowed some Wall Street firms to offer coins to clients. There is a computerized trading network, and the market can rise or dip as much as 20 percent in a few weeks. Thus, thousands of dollars are made and lost daily in the fluctuating coin market. It is a fact—coins are big business! Millions of Americans are part-time and full-time numismatists. But as with many hard assets, there are counterfeit and altered coins (and art and stamps). A buyer must beware. Buy collectibles that are accompanied by proper certification and authentication. *Insure your collectibles.*

When insuring your collectibles, you will need to get a separate "rider" to your homeowner's policy for these items. These items are not usually covered by standard homeowner's or renter's insurance. In most cases collectibles and jewelry are insured only up to a nominal amount such as $250 on a general policy. Do not make the mistake of believing that these items are covered and discovering otherwise after loss or destruction has occurred. Discuss these items with your insurance carrier, obtain appropriate appraisals if necessary, and carry the proper amount of insurance.

Similarly, since the invention of the first postage stamp by the British, the hobby of stamp collecting has grown steadily larger and larger. Even during the Great Depression when the stock market took its most dramatic plunge, stamps retained their value, and many people found the funds to purchase them. In the late 1980s investors have actively entered the field of philately (stamp collecting), but as inflation moderated, stamp values declined.

For example, during 1989 a block of four U.S. 24-cent 1918 Airmail Inverts sold for $1 million, but in a 2001 retail guide the same block was listed for only $600,000. Contrary to Lieutenant Kojak's remark on a television series, a stamp is not merely "a piece of gum paper." The philatelic market is open to anyone who wishes to buy and sell stamps, but the stamp market is complex and moves up and down. For example, a 1906 2¢ Philippine issue retailed in 2001 at only 35¢, but a carmine red 1846, Annapolis, Maryland Postmasters' Provisional issue retailed in 2001 at $200,000. Stamp firms employ hundreds of personnel to satisfy the needs of the collector or investor, and all must agree that stamps are big business.

Investors seem to move from one hard asset to another. For example, in the early 1980s, investors flocked into investment-grade diamonds. Flawless, D, one-carat stone prices went through the roof. Then the market crashed. A similar scenario occurred with the stamp market with certain investment-promoted stamps.

Before considering an investment in hard assets, you must understand the basic concept of opportunity cost. An investment is not worthwhile economically unless it appears that the rate of return from the investment will be at least equal to what could have been earned from other investment alternatives in the same risk category (stocks, bonds, real estate, or commodities). That is, the potential income from an investment must equal or exceed any potential income from an alternative investment before such investment is worthwhile. An investor should consider the risk from robbery, the expenses of keeping hard assets, and the interest that might have been earned from an alternative investment. Remember that hard assets don't pay cash dividends or interest.

You should be intimately familiar with the hard asset before you invest a great deal of capital. Buy quality collectibles and keep your expenses, such as commissions and overhead expenses, as low as possible. Diversify, diversify and diversify. The markups are high, and you must liquidate at wholesale prices. There are many unscrupulous dealers. But if you insist, keep the following concept in mind: "soft hands" and "hard hands." A collector/investor normally holds onto collectibles until he or she dies. The collector is "hard hands." But at death, the collectible falls into "soft hands" (surviving spouses, children). The soft hands people know little about the collectible and probably wish to sell. They'll sell cheap—near wholesale or below. Buy only from "soft hand" people for the best profit. Do not use leveraging techniques, and speculate only with money you can afford to lose.

23

WHEN TO SELL AN INVESTMENT

Most people enjoy talking about what to buy. There's usually no shortage of investment advice from professionals, colleagues, relatives, friends, and acquaintances—however, rarely does anyone talk about when to sell. Perhaps the reason for the relative silence on this crucial subject is that selling is often a more difficult decision than buying.

Why are many investors unable to make wise selling decisions? In the case of investments that perform poorly, selling requires acceptance of the fact that the prior decision to buy was a mistake. Most people are reluctant to admit that they made a mistake. On the other hand, selling a successful investment can be just as difficult as selling a poor investment.

Four factors explain why investors avoid selling successful investments:

1. Selling a successful investment generally results in additional taxable income and higher taxes; thus, not selling a successful investment minimizes tax liability. Currently, the tax laws provide for lower tax rates on gains resulting from long-term capital investments. Even then, however, a significant amount of taxes may be owed.

2. A second factor that discourages investors from selling successful investments is psychological attachment. After holding an investment, such as a piece of property, for an extended period of time, an investor may develop a genuine fondness for

the item. After spending time searching for the ideal property to buy, inspecting it periodically after acquisition, and perhaps developing it, many investors are reluctant to turn their "baby" over to someone else.

3. A third factor is greed. For example, when a stock investment is increasing in value, the investor who hopes to sell at the absolute peak price will probably hold the investment too long.

4. A fourth factor is laziness or forgetfulness. People often forget about an investment. An investor must keep track of his or her investments in order to maximize gains and minimize losses.

The key to knowing when to sell any investment is to plan in advance. For unsuccessful investments, set a "stop-loss" point, such as a decline of 20 percent. In the stock market, fluctuations of 10 percent are fairly common; consequently price increases or declines in this range should be expected. In the event an investment ultimately declines to the stop-loss point, an investor should sell unless there are some compelling reasons to keep it.

In the case of successful investments, you should plan to sell when predetermined objectives are achieved. You should set investment goals such as a 25 percent increase over purchase price. When the investment reaches your appreciation goal, you should make a fresh evaluation of the investment just as you did when it was initially acquired. Is there a good reason not to sell? In other words, is there a sound basis for setting a new price appreciation objective? If you do not sell, you should set a new stop-loss point or investment goal based on the current price, not the initial purchase price.

24

DISABILITY PROTECTION

Just like death, incapacity or legal incompleteness is something no one wants to think about. Key 13 covers the safety net of disability insurance, but disability planning includes living wills and powers of attorney in case of an automobile accident or a sudden or gradual disease (for example, Alzheimer's disease).

A *power of attorney* is a legal document whereby a person gives another person the right to handle all or part of his or her assets. In effect, the other person can act as your substitute in case you are unable to act for yourself with respect to a legal, financial, or real estate matter. This technique is especially appropriate for younger people in special circumstances (for instance, being out of the country for a period of time) and elderly individuals. At the beginning of this century, 25 percent of the population of the United States was over the age of 65.

A person or institution may have your power of attorney to do almost anything, from signing your check to running your small business. There are several types of powers of attorney:

1. General power of attorney
2. Specific power of attorney
3. Durable power of attorney
4. Springing power of attorney

The general power of attorney may be the trickiest. In this instance, the principal nominates another person (the agent or attorney-in-fact) to act on the principal's behalf. Many times, the spouse is named as the attorney-in-fact. Often, there may be more than one agent (for example, spouse and a child), so the formal document should clearly state whether the named agents are authorized to act separately or must act jointly. This traditional power of attorney can be revoked at any time while the principal is competent. The document terminates when the principal dies or becomes incompetent.

A specific power of attorney gives only a limited power, as outlined in the document. For example, a taxpayer can grant a specific power of attorney to a representative who will represent the taxpayer before the IRS by using IRS Form 2848 or Form 8868. The latter gives less authority to the designated representative, so Form 8868 should be considered whenever possible. A power of attorney may be granted without using Form 2848, but all information that would normally be provided on the IRS form must be given. A representative who does not file the form may be prohibited from receiving or inspecting certain tax information.

To be considered valid, a tax power of attorney must contain certain information about you. This includes your name, Social Security or taxpayer identification number, and address. If a joint return is being filed and both spouses are naming the same representative, the identical information must be provided for the spouse. Your representative's name, Central Authorization File (CAF) number (if already assigned), address, and telephone number must be designated. The IRS assigns the CAF number after your representative files a Form 2848 or Form 8868 with an IRS office.

A durable power of attorney allows the power to remain in effect after the principal becomes incompetent. Durable powers permit individuals to avoid guardianship by establishing noncourt regimes for the management of their affairs in the event of later incompetency. Think of it as a senility insurance comparable to that available to relatively wealthy people who use funded revocable trusts for the same purpose.

Sometimes called a "living will," a durable power of attorney allows a named person to make health care decisions for you and to give medical consent if you are unable to do so. You may give instructions that no heroic measures may be taken to prolong your life, or if you have a terminal condition, you may provide instructions in advance not to prolong your life if there is no hope.

Most states and the District of Columbia recognize a durable power of attorney. Generally, the document should contain a durability clause such as follows:

This power of attorney shall not be affected by the subsequent disability or incompetence of the principal.

The principal's signature should be witnessed or acknowledged by a notary public. A durability clause will allow a person to avoid a court proceeding in the event of Alzheimer's disease or some other incapacitating illness.

About 20 states, including New York, California, and Michigan, recognize a special type of durable power of attorney called a *springing power of attorney*—the power of attorney "springs" into effect when a specified event occurs. These springing powers allow a person to maintain control over his or her affairs as long as possible. For example, the general or specific power of attorney remains dormant unless you become physically or mentally incompetent or you enter a nursing home.

In states not recognizing springing powers, similar results can still be achieved. Have your attorney draft a document with the executed power together with a letter specifying that the power of attorney is to be released upon the occurrence of certain events.

25

RETIREMENT PLANNING

The earlier you begin to plan for retirement, the more you can solidify your financial position. You'll need a solid nest egg of retirement investments to allow you to grow old gracefully. When many people reach retirement age, they are financially unprepared; yet they may live 20 to 30 percent of their entire life span after retirement.

As a starting point, assume that you will need about 80 percent of your regular income to live comfortably in your later years. Although some of your expenses (such as taxes) will fall, other expenses (such as medical expenses) will increase.

Tax-deferred Keogh plans and IRAs may be used in your retirement planning to take advantage of the power of compounding interest. Self-employed individuals are permitted to set up qualified retirement plans. A self-employed person may deduct from gross taxable income an annual contribution to a Keogh defined contribution plan that is limited to the smaller of $40,000 or 25 percent of earned income. For example, suppose Johnson owns a real estate firm that nets $40,000 (*after the Keogh contribution*). The maximum contribution to a defined contribution Keogh pension plan that is deductible from adjusted gross income is $10,000 (25 percent × $40,000). Technically, you can contribute 20 percent of gross earned income or 25 percent of the net earned income (*after the Keogh contribution*). Here Johnson can deduct 25 percent of $40,000 (X =

.25[$50,000 − X]) or 20 percent of *gross* earned income of $50,000 ($40,000 + 10,000).

You may use a Keogh plan if you earn income as an independent contractor or from a sideline business. An individual can contribute to a Keogh plan even while participating in a corporate pension plan elsewhere as an employee. Earned income refers to salary, professional fees, and book royalties and sales but does not include passive income items such as dividends or interest. Earned income is reduced by contributions to qualified, plans on that individual's behalf.

Sample Keogh contributions are shown in Exhibit 25.1. It is assumed that the annual contributions at the end of the year are $7,500 and $15,000, with the investment fund earning 10 and 15 percent, compounded annually. For example, an annual contribution of $7,500 for 30 years will total $1,233,705 at 10 percent interest. Thus, a Keogh retirement plan is a great tax shelter and savings vehicle for an individual.

EXHIBIT 25.1
Keogh Plan Accumulations

	At 10% Growth Rate		At 15% Growth Rate	
	Annual Contribution	Annual Contribution	Annual Contribution	Annual Contribution
	$7,500	$15,000	$7,500	$15,000
Year	Value at End of Period		Value at End of Period	
10	$119,527	$239,055	$152,277	$304,554
20	429,562	859,125	768,327	1,536,654
30	1,233,705	2,467,410	3,260,587	6,521,175

Self-employed individuals not covered by another qualified plan can establish a tax-deductible IRA subject to a limit of the smaller of $3,000 (for 2002 through 2004) or 100 percent of compensation. Catch-up contributions may be made by individuals age 50 and over.

Neither the taxpayer nor spouse may be active participants in any qualified plan to benefit fully. If the taxpayer or spouse is an active participant in another
qualified plan, the IRA deduction limitation is phased
out proportionately between certain adjusted gross
income (AGI) ranges, taking into account any passive
losses and taxable Social Security benefits and ignoring
any foreign income exclusion and the IRA deduction
(see Exhibit 25.2).

EXHIBIT 25.2
Phase-out of IRA Deductibility (2002)

AGI Filing Status	Phase-out Begins	Phase-out Ends
Single and head of household	$34,000	$44,000
Married, filing joint return	54,000	64,000
Married, filing separate return	-0-	10,000

Nondeductible contributions can be made to a traditional IRA, subject to the same dollar limits for
deductible contributions of $3,000 of earned income
(for 2002 through 2004). Taxpayers who make nondeductible IRA contributions are required to complete
and file Form 8606 with their tax returns. Income in the
account accumulates tax-free until distributed. Only the
account earnings will be taxed upon distribution. A taxpayer may elect to treat deductible IRA contributions as
nondeductible. If an individual has no taxable income
for the year after taking into account other deductions,
the election would be beneficial. Such designation is to
be made on the individual's tax return for the taxable
year to which the designation relates.

The amazing amounts that can be accumulated in two
IRAs by a working couple are indicated in Exhibit 25.3.
These figures assume $4,000 is deposited at the end of
each year with annual compounding rates of 10, 12, and

15 percent. For example, during a period of 30 years, a total of $657,976 can be accumulated in a couple's IRAs at an annual compounding rate of 10 percent. The earning power of compound interest in a tax-deferred retirement account is formidable.

EXHIBIT 25.3
IRA Accumulations Based on $4,000 Annual Contribution ($2,000 each for husband and wife)

Number of Years Contributed	10%	12%	15%
10	$63,748	$70,195	$81,212
20	229,100	288,208	409,774
30	657,976	965,328	1,738,980
40	1,770,372	3,068,364	7,116,360

Note: Maximum annual dollar contribution limits for a single IRA were changed by Congress in 2001 as follows: $3,000 in 2002–2004, $4,000 in 2005–2007, and $4,000 in 2008.

A participant has a zero basis in tax-deductible contributions to an IRA because they are not currently taxed. Once retirement payments are received, such payments are ordinary income and are not subject to the ten-year averaging allowed for lump-sum distributions. The value of undistributed proceeds of an IRA account is excluded from the participant's gross estate if the proceeds are payable as an annuity to a beneficiary (other than the estate). Payments made to a participant before age $59\frac{1}{2}$ are subject to a nondeductible 10 percent penalty tax on such actual, or constructive payments.

A Keogh or traditional IRA (and Roth IRA) participant may make a deductible contribution for a tax year up to the time prescribed for filing the individual's tax return, including any filing extensions. However, a Keogh plan must have been established by December 31 to qualify for a deductible contribution in the subsequent year. For example, an individual can establish a Keogh plan by December 31 by placing a small amount in the plan. A much larger contribution can then be made in the next year up to the time prescribed for filing the individual's tax return (including any extensions). By contrast, an individual can establish and fund an IRA or Simplified Employee Pension Plan (SEP) after the end of the year and still receive a deductible contribution for the prior year.

A traditional IRA or qualified plan may be rolled over to avoid taxation of a lump-sum distribution or termination distribution. A distribution is not included in gross income if it is transferred within 60 days to an IRA or other qualified plan. Further, any rollover amount in an IRA can be rolled over later into another qualified plan if the IRA consists of only the amounts from the original qualified plan. Remember: Distributions from an IRA are not eligible for capital gains treatment and ten-year averaging treatment.

IRA and Keogh participants may self-direct their investments into a wide variety of assets even though the assets are controlled by a trustee or custodian. The acquisition by an IRA or self-directed Keogh or corporate plan of collectibles (art, gems, paintings, metals) is treated as a distribution (is subject to taxation). For an IRA or Keogh participant under age $59^1/_2$, there is also a 10 percent premature distribution penalty.

An alternative to the traditional IRA is the non-deductible Roth IRA. Although amounts contributed to a Roth IRA are not tax deductible, earnings inside a Roth IRA are not taxable, and all qualified distributions from a Roth IRA are tax-free. If an individual plans to meet the five-year holding period and keep the funds in the account for at least 18 to 20 years, a Roth IRA is probably better than a traditional IRA. If a 15-year-old person begins to contribute $2,000 to a Roth IRA, in 50 years the Roth IRA will be worth around $235,000 (assuming an annual rate of return of 10 percent).

Another alternative to the traditional qualified retirement plan is a Simplified Employee Pension Plan (SEP). A company may establish an SEP for its employees, or self-employed persons and partnerships may establish SEPs. Current contribution limits are the lesser of 15 percent of compensation or $40,000.

Many individuals contribute up to $11,000 (in 2002) to a Section 401(k) retirement plan. Such a plan allows participants to elect either to receive up to $11,000 (in 2002) in cash (taxed currently) or to have a contribution made on their behalf to a profit-sharing or stock bonus plan. An individual should contribute as much as possible as soon as possible to tax-deferred retirement plans.

Many 401(k) plans have age and work requirements. It is good idea to find out these requirements up front. Usually the requirements will be something to the effect of "the employee must be at least 21 years of age and have six months of service with the company." Many employers will match a portion of employee contributions. This is a good way to earn extra money that is tax deferred. See the chart below for how this would work for an employee who has a salary of $50,000 per year that works for a company that will match employee contributions 50 percent on the first 6 percent donated by the employee.

Employee %	Employee Contribution	Employer %	Employer Contribution	Total tax deferred	Total Compensation
0%	$0	0%	$0	$0	$50,000
4%	$2,000	2%	$1,000	$3,000	$51,000
6%	$3,000	3%	$1,500	$4,500	$51,500
10%	$5,000	3%	$1,500	$6,500	$51,500

There are other important things to know about 401(k) plans. The first is that it is similar to an IRA or a Keogh in that there is a tax penalty if money is withdrawn before age $59^1/_2$ or unless you become disabled. One advantage of a 401(k) plan is that if money is needed, a loan can be taken out against the amount in your plan and the amount is paid back with interest. Although, this is not recommended, it is possible that this type of loan could become necessary for items such as unforeseen medical expenses, or other exigencies.

When changing jobs you can usually take your 401(k) savings with you to your new job by completing a rollover form. Make sure you do a rollover. Do not remove the money from your old plan because that would cause an early withdrawal penalty. The human resources department at your employer can usually assist with these changes. In some cases, you may not want to move your money to a new plan. Find out from the company that you are leaving if you are able to leave your money in their plan. In many cases you will be able to do this. If your new employer does not have a plan or if you determine that a different investment strategy is right for you, conversion to a Roth IRA may be a possibility. Keep in mind that this has tax consequences upon conversion, so you must ensure that cash is available to pay your taxes when this type of transaction is done. Nonprofit organizations may have 403(b) plans. In essence, this works like a 401(k) plan, but the specifics of any plan should be discussed with your human resources department or plan administrator to ensure that you have a full understanding of the costs and benefits of these retirement plans.

For more information see Barron's *Keys to Retirement Planning* by Warren Boroson.

26

SOCIAL SECURITY

Most people work at least 40 hours a week and every 2 weeks or once a month get paid for the work they have done. When you look at your paycheck, you are concerned primarily with the bottom line—the net amount, or take-home pay. Few people consider computing their paycheck to see if the employer has properly calculated the various deductions and net pay.

Today, payroll administration is more complex than ever before. Even though payroll software packages are being used by most firms, people still must enter the data. Occasionally, human errors occur. Furthermore, even computerized systems sometimes develop glitches in their programming. A good idea is to occasionally verify the computations associated with your paycheck.

Social Security is one of the most significant deductions from your gross pay. Since Social Security tax is a major deduction, you should know how it is computed and what benefits it provides. Virtually every working individual has Social Security tax withheld from his or her paycheck. This tax was established to fund a government program that provides for the economic security and social welfare of the American worker and his or her family.

The Social Security tax is also known as FICA (Federal Income Contribution Act) tax. The FICA tax rate in 2002 was 15.3 percent, of which the Medicare portion is 2.9 percent; thus, the Social Security portion is 12.4 percent. This tax amount (rate) is divided equally between the employee and the employer. Regarding Social Security, for instance, the employee has 6.2

percent of gross earnings withheld from his or her pay. The company/employer is responsible for paying the remaining 6.2 percent. Social Security tax is applied to every dollar earned up to a maximum amount called the base amount. In 2002 this base amount was $84,900. The Medicare portion of 2.9 percent is applied to all earnings (that is, no maximum amount); one half of this amount is paid by the employer and one half by the employee.

Benefits that a worker may expect to receive after paying the employee's portion of the FICA tax during working years fall into four categories:

1. Old age or disability benefits paid to the individual worker
2. Benefits paid to the dependents of a retired or disabled worker
3. Benefits paid to surviving family members of a deceased worker
4. Lump-sum death payments

With each of these, once eligibility requirements have been met, an individual may immediately begin receiving benefits.

Benefits received are based on an employee's average monthly wage. There are a few situations in which benefits may be denied. For instance, a retired employee may earn more than a prescribed amount or an individual may be convicted of certain crimes. To apply for benefits, you should go to your local Social Security office.

Every three or four years you should obtain Form 7004 from the Social Security Administration. Fill out the form, send it in, and after about 30 days the government will tell you the amount of your earnings since 1950. They also will tell you your estimated retirement benefits and your estimated disability benefits. This preventive action on your part can catch any errors in your

Social Security account and help you plan for your retirement.

For more information see Barron's *Keys to Understanding Social Security Benefits* by Tom Dickens and D. Larry Crumbley.

27

PENSION AND PROFIT-SHARING PLANS

Tax-deferred retirement plans are the ultimate wealth builder and tax shelter. U.S. tax law provides favored tax treatment to qualified retirement plans. Your employer gets an immediate tax deduction for contributions to the plan, but you are not taxed on the contributions until the benefits are received. The employer contribution goes to a trust that is exempt from taxation. Thus, just as with a Keogh plan or an IRA, you receive the benefits of tax-deferred compounding interest.

The types of retirement plans available to individuals having earned income are as follows:

1. For employees of ordinary business and Sub-chapter S corporations:
   - Pension plans
   - Profit-sharing plans
   - Stock bonus plans
   - Employee stock ownership plans
   - Simplified employee pension plans (SEPs)
2. For employees of partnerships:
   - Pension plans
   - Profit-sharing plans
   - SEPs
3. For proprietors and partners (Keogh plans):
   - Pension plans
   - Profit-sharing plans
   - SEPs

4. For some individuals who have earned income:
  • Individual retirement accounts

All these types of plans, if "qualified," give immediate deductions to the payor of contributions and deferral of taxable income to the recipient (see Key 25 for a discussion of Keogh plans and IRAs).

The foregoing types of plans also fit within one of two categories—defined *contribution* plans and defined *benefit* plans. For each category there are limitations imposed on the amounts of benefits and contributions.

In a defined *contribution* plan, the employer's contributions are fixed, but the amount of the employee's pension is not. In a defined *benefit* plan, the amount of the employee's pension is set, but the employer's contribution is not. Defined *contribution* plans include profit-sharing plans, money-purchase pension plans, target benefit plans, stock bonus plans, employee stock ownership plans, and individual retirement accounts.

Today, the only type of defined benefit plan is the regular pension plan. A defined benefit plan is more difficult to administer, and the fees associated with it are considerably higher.

There are three types of qualified retirement plans: pension, profit-sharing, and stock bonus plans.

A pension plan is one under which the amount of retirement benefits is determined and then the required amount of annual contributions is actuarially computed. A pension plan is a plan established and maintained by an employer primarily to provide systematically for the payment of definitely determinable benefits to employees over a period of years, usually for life, after retirement. Retirement benefits generally are measured by, and based on, such factors as years of service and compensation received by the employees. The determination of the amount of retirement benefits and the contributions to provide such benefits are not dependent upon corporate profits.

110

A profit-sharing plan is designed not to provide a fixed amount of monthly retirement income but rather to provide a fund, built up out of contributions from annual profits or accumulated profits of an employer, that will be available to the employee later, usually on retirement. A profit-sharing plan is established and maintained by an employer to provide for the participation in profits by the employees or their beneficiaries. The plan must provide a definite predetermined formula for allocating the contributions made to the plan among the participants and for distributing the funds accumulated under the plan after a fixed number of years, the attainment of a stated age, or upon the prior occurrence of some event such as layoff, illness, disability, retirement, death, or severance of employment. Separate accounts are maintained for each participant.

A stock bonus plan is a plan established and maintained by an employer to provide benefits similar to those of a profit-sharing plan, except that the contributions by the employer are not necessarily dependent upon profits, and the benefits are distributable in stock of the employer company. For the purpose of allocating and distributing the stock that is to be shared among the employees or their beneficiaries, such a plan is subject to the same requirements as a profit-sharing plan.

A cafeteria benefit plan may be established to give an employee the option to receive a current salary payment or to have a stipulated amount contributed on his or her behalf to a profit-sharing plan. Such plans under Section 401(k) generally must satisfy the pension-plan qualification rules, and these plans must not permit the distribution of amounts attributable to employer contributions merely because of a stated period of plan participation or a passage of a fixed period of time. In general, employees may contribute as much as 15 percent of their annual salary up to a maximum of $11,000 in 2002.

A Section 401(k) Plan permits a participant to elect

to receive up to $11,000 (in 2002) in cash or have a contribution made to a profit-sharing plan or a stock bonus plan. Many employees fail to take advantage of their 401(k) plan. A twenty-five-year-old person earning $25,000 can accumulate $797,788 in a 401(k) plan, retiring at age 62, by making 6 percent annual contributions, with an investment return of 8 percent, and a salary growing only 4 percent each year. Young people should not put much of their monies in the most conservative funds (such as, money markets).

An employee stock ownership plan (ESOP) is a defined benefit plan in the form of a trust. An ESOP is created by an employer corporation for the benefit of its employees. The trust is funded by the transfer to it of stock of the employer corporation or of an affiliate, which is usually the parent. The primary purpose of an ESOP is to broaden the ownership by employees of common stock in the employer corporation; the secondary purpose is to provide a retirement fund. Since a corporation can contribute stock rather than cash, there is no cash flow drain, and the corporation receives a tax deduction equal to the fair market value of stock.

Quite often a plan participant has a choice of how the retirement funds are to be invested (safe, guaranteed income instruments or exotic risky investments). In general, you want to maximize long-term returns with minimum risk to principal. Thus, precious metals, futures, and options trading are out. Since losses cannot be recognized on investments in a retirement account, leveraged tax incentive investments (real estate and energy) are not appropriate.

The most appropriate investments for your retirement account are fixed-income and equity-type investments. The younger you are, the more aggressive you can be (you can select riskier investments), because you still have the opportunity to recover from a bad investment. One suggestion is to maintain a percentage of retirement assets equal to your age in conservative assets (such as, CDs or bonds). Invest the remainder in assets likely to provide a higher return over time. In any case, maintain a diversified portfolio. Do not place all of your eggs in one basket. Over time, stock investments provide a substantially higher return than bonds, and bonds provide a higher return than cash equivalents.

28

ESTATE PLANNING

Everyone needs an estate plan. People have many excuses for not planning their estate: complexity, costs, indecision, or merely procrastination. Whether you are a business owner, an employee, or self-employed, whether you have substantial wealth or are of modest means, *you should plan your estate*. Estate planning includes building an estate during a lifetime, then seeing that those assets are protected in an estate that can be passed to the next generation.

Estate planning is the art of designing a program for the effective enjoyment, management, and disposition of property at the minimum possible tax cost. This process is much more than just planning for death. Building an estate throughout life should be part of the estate planning process. Estate planning tries to encourage a wealth-building approach for everyone and considers income tax, fiduciary tax, estate tax, and gift tax to minimize the overall tax burden of the total family unit.

Anyone with income, property, and investments must be concerned with estate planning. It may be even more important to the owner of a medium-sized estate than to the owner of a large estate, because the waste of a single asset in such an estate could prevent the accomplishment of objectives and bring hardship to the family unit. In other words, everyone who owns assets needs an estate plan, whether it involves a simple will or a complex arrangement of several of the estate planning devices available to the estate's owner, such as a trust, charitable contributions, and life insurance.

There is a human side to estate planning. How much wealth should be left to children? Warren Buffett, a Nebraska billionaire, believes the right amount to leave children is "enough money so that they would feel they could do anything but not so much they could do nothing." Buffett suggests that only a few thousand dollars should be left to a college graduate.

Many professional skills are useful in the estate planning process. Usually, a team effort works best. The attorney, the accountant (CPA), the trust officer, and the life insurance underwriter are the professionals most often associated with the team. You may also include a member of the growing profession of Certified Financial Planners.

Before an estate plan becomes effective, the appropriate legal documents must be executed. The necessity for careful planning and execution of the legal documents cannot be overemphasized, for faulty execution is a sure way of altering or even invalidating any estate plan. These legal instruments must be drafted by a competent attorney who is well versed in estate planning techniques. Do not assume that any attorney can draft a will. A specialist in, say, real estate is probably not conversant with the latest developments in estate work.

All estate planning documents should be reviewed periodically to assure that they continue to express the objectives of the estate owner. A periodic review of your financial status and family relationships should be undertaken to determine if there have been any changes that necessitate a revision of the estate plan. For example, a divorce generally necessitates a change in a person's will. In addition, an estate plan should be reviewed in the light of any changes or potential changes in the relevant estate or tax laws. Such a review could bring about a modification in the plan that would produce significant benefits to the estate owner, while the neglect of such a review could be very costly.

Since the time of death is uncertain, everyone, young or old, should plan for the contingency of death. Even with the great advances in modern medicine, not everyone is lucky enough to grow old gracefully. Why build an estate and allow much of it to go to the federal government through estate taxes?

29

A WILL IS IMPORTANT

Every individual should have a will. The will is a key vehicle of transfer at death, and its preparation is often the first step taken by people in planning the disposition of their estates. A will is a set of written instructions prepared under legal rules that directs how a person's property will be disposed of at death. Everyone needs a properly executed will, and a copy of the will should be kept outside the safe deposit box. If the only copy is inside the box, it may be impossible for the heirs or executors to get at it without a lot of time-consuming legal rigmarole.

Stories are legion about the disastrous consequences of dying without a will, called *intestate*. In such a situation, the state laws direct how the assets will be distributed—a will by default. The county or state probate court will appoint an administrator, who may not be qualified to manage your estate. Most intestate succession laws favor the surviving spouse, child, or grandchildren. Assets, therefore, might go to children of a previous marriage, to distant nephews and nieces, or even to enemies. The estate process can drag on for many years, and the lawyer(s) may get the bulk of the estate assets.

If you don't have a will, in effect you're allowing the state to draft a will for you after your death and to decide who administers it—quite possibly a stranger. Most state laws assume that family members (and not friends) are the natural objects of one's bounty. Without a will, friends are left out. State laws work in many cases, but a will provides for a much more efficient and financially beneficial distribution of one's assets. If you have specific items you wish to leave to particular family members or friends, a will is essential. In any case, why force your family or friends to decide how you want your estate distributed? A will is a thoughtful gesture to those you love and may save them from unnecessary squabbles.

Young and old need a will. Young people do not necessarily live to old age. Statistics provide grim reminders that death often comes unexpectedly. For instance, over 30,000 people are killed each year in alcohol-related traffic accidents.

Your will should designate an executor, who will be responsible for the administration of your estate after your death. Your will can include a provision to waive the bond required from an executor. This waiver may result in cost savings, because a premium must be paid by the executor to obtain the bond. Also, your will can contain a simultaneous death provision. Where there is insufficient evidence to determine which spouse predeceased the other in a common accident, this clause specifies the survivor.

Wills and estate plans are not once-in-a-lifetime documents. People outgrow their initial wills, and new laws make revision of wills essential. Also, amendments or revisions are necessary in case of marriage, divorce, birth of a child, death of a spouse or child, marriage of a child, increase or decrease in personal wealth, a move to a new state, or purchase of life insurance. Thus, estate planning is a lifelong process.

If a person runs a business, the will should make provision for the operation of the business after his or her death. In some states an executor cannot lawfully continue a business without a specific authorization. The business operation may come to a halt, buildings may deteriorate, or the business may have to be liquidated if proper authority is not given. Thus, key provisions in the will should cover issues such as valuation of the business, succession, and disposal.

The will is used to designate heirs, to identify the property they are to receive, to indicate the person (or institution) who will act as executor or executrix of the estate, and to clarify similar details. A useful provision related to the will is the marital deduction. The basic advantage of using the marital deduction is the favorable tax consequences. The cost of this tax savings, however, may be the compromise of the estate owner's objectives, the possible deferred increase in transfer costs, or the loss of control of an asset.

Married couples with small estates may wish to have a simple "I love you will." Here each spouse leaves all of his or her assets to the surviving spouse. Even in such cases, however, it is necessary that a legal arrangement be made for the assets to be left in a trust for any minor children in case both parties die simultaneously (as in a plane accident). In legal terms, a holographic will is in one's own handwriting, and a nuncupative will is oral. An oral will is seldom valid, and in some states the unwitnessed holographic will is not valid.

Before a will is accepted for probate, the probate court determines whether the will is legal in substance and form. Generally, the testator (male) or testatrix (female) must sign the will in the presence of a specific number of witnesses. Two credible witnesses are necessary in most states, but three are required in South Carolina and Vermont. Credible means that the witness must be a competent person who can legally testify in a court.

The testator must not have been under undue influence and should be supervised by an authoritative party, such as an attorney. The will must be in a single document and must include an attestation clause, which is a single item before the testator's signature indicating that the testator signed the will in the presence of the appropriate number of witnesses and that the witnesses were present to witness the testator's signature. Be sure to destroy all of the draft copies of the final executed will.

A person may wish to specify in the will if they wish to be cremated or donate body parts to medical science for research. Anyone who is the parent or guardian of children under the age of eighteen should appoint a guardian of the minor's property. Appointment of a guardian by will avoids the filing of a surety bond by the guardian with the court. In essence, a will expresses the final wishes of the testator.

A codicil is an instrument that revokes, changes, or adds to the terms of a will. A joint will is one document that is signed by husband and wife. A living will is a separate document in which a person expresses a wish that his or her life not be prolonged by artificial or extraordinary measures.

Briefly summarized in the following paragraphs are two other types of wills designed to provide adequately for surviving spouse and children while minimizing estate taxes.

Assume that the husband dies first. In a two-part will, some assets pass directly to the surviving wife, with a minimum pecuniary amount specified (for instance, a will might state that no less than $400,000 is to go directly to the wife). She controls these assets. The remaining assets, up to the federal *exemption equivalent* ($1 million in 2002 and 2003), go into a bypass trust, so that they will not be taxed in the wife's estate either. If there are still assets left over beyond the exemption equivalent amount, they go directly to the wife and qualify for the unlimited marital deduction.

In a three-part will, some assets go directly to the surviving wife, who controls them. Again, a minimum pecuniary amount may be specified. Also, as in the two-part will, some property goes directly to a bypass trust, up to the exemption equivalent. The remaining property passes to a qualified terminable interest property (QTIP) trust, which provides income to the wife for life and gives the property to children at the wife's death. This area is very technical, and a reader should discuss such a trust with a competent attorney.

Of course, the kind of will that is best for a given person depends on the individual situation and may change as the person's circumstances change. Planning is necessary to avoid creating an unintended heir of your estate: Uncle Sam (see Key 28).

30

PRENUPTIAL
AGREEMENTS

One major way of obtaining wealth is through marriage, and some people do look for a wealthy spouse. How can a wealthy person or family protect their riches from such a person? One way is by means of a premarital contract. But prenuptial agreements are not just for the rich.

Every 27 seconds or so, someone in the United States gets divorced. The United States has the highest divorce rate in the world—almost twice as high as many other affluent countries. Yet in the two crucial human decisions—to marry and divorce—knowledge and reason play the smallest part.

Most courts are beginning to accept prenuptial agreements, but 11 states limit enforcement to property rights. These states hold waivers of alimony and support void as against public policy: California, Colorado, Illinois, Indiana, Iowa, Kentucky, Minnesota, Ohio, Oklahoma, Oregon, and Washington.

A *prenuptial agreement* is simply an agreement between a man and a woman entered into before marriage, which may range from several to 30 pages. Costs can be as high as $5,000 in lawyer fees. Such an agreement is also called an *antenuptial agreement* or a *premarital agreement*. The main purpose of this agreement is to decide who gets what in case the marriage is dissolved for some reason. If a premarital agreement is not set up, the court divides the property as it sees fit. Sometimes what the court views as fair may not be the same as what the two parties view as fair.

When a court divides your property, it first looks to see what property is nonmarital and what is equitable distribution property. Equitable distribution property is acquired after marriage, except for a gift that is intended solely for the use of one party. For example, a parent's check made out to one spouse as a gift is viewed as nonmarital property. After dividing the property into nonmarital and equitable distribution property, the court divides the equitable distribution property "fairly" as seen by the court.

Each state has its own rules regarding the division of property, but if you marry and have an agreement drawn up in one state and then move to another state to live, the rules of the state of residence may weigh more heavily than the state where the agreement was drawn. If a move is being planned after the wedding, the agreement should probably be drawn in the state in which you plan to live.

Most states require both parties to disclose all assets to one another before entering into the agreement. If the partners fail to make full disclosure, the agreement can be considered void. The courts look to see if the agreement is equitable. There must be no evidence of fraud, duress, or overreaching. Before signing the agreement, both parties should have a reasonable opportunity to seek counsel.

Valid reasons exist for a person to have such an agreement prepared. For example, a party may specify that each spouse is responsible for any taxes that were not paid before the marriage. This clause protects you in the event that the IRS tries to recover unpaid taxes owed by your spouse.

Another reason to have a prenuptial agreement is that with divorce rates on the rise, many men and women are marrying for a second or third time; often these marriages include children from a previous marriage. By having a premarital agreement, each party knows ahead of time how the children will be cared for. Or two young professionals, an attorney and a doctor, may wish to protect the valuation of their businesses.

Also, many retired people are getting married and may have acquired a great deal of wealth through the years. There is a risk that one party simply may be looking for money.

You should understand the tax consequences of entering into such an agreement, especially the impact on federal estate tax (see Key 28).

Prenuptial agreements should not be signed at the last minute before a marriage. Coercion, duress, or failure of full disclosure are grounds for invalidating a prenuptial. Each party should review and sign the agreement, and both parties should probably have different lawyers. Videotaping the signing can be helpful.

The agreement could be dissolved after a certain number of years (for instance, 20). If both parties agree, the prenuptial can be revoked at any time.

31

USING TRUSTS

A trust is a fiduciary relationship in which one party holds property, subject to an equitable obligation to keep or use such property for the benefit of another person. However, the IRS's number one enforcement target today is the so-called *abusive trust*—ones used to avoid tax on normal income. Plus, trusts that receive income will be taxed at higher rates than individuals.

In a trust, legal ownership is divorced from equitable ownership, and legal title is held by the trustee exclusively for the benefit of the beneficiary because of the latter's equitable interest. At least one court has defined a trust as a property right held by one party for the use of another.

A trust is a relationship with respect to property held by the trustee. Such property is referred to as the trust property and may be defined as the interest in a thing—real or personal, tangible or intangible—that the trustee holds, subject to the rights of another. Aside from the trust property, the relationship usually involves three parties:

- The *settlor* (or grantor) creates or intentionally causes the trust to come into existence.
- The *beneficiary* is the person entitled to the benefits from the trust property.
- The third party to the trust is the *trustee*, who holds the legal title to the trust property for the benefit of the beneficiary.

In a fiduciary relationship, the law demands that one party must have an unusually high standard of ethical or moral conduct with respect to another party of the relationship. In a trust, the trustee is the one required to have such characteristics. Trustees, whether individual or institutional, must represent and act solely in the interest of the beneficiaries; they are not permitted to consider their own personal needs or desires. Because of the nature of a trust, the trustee is expected to apply more than casual consideration and judgment in dealings with the beneficiary. Being a trustee is serious business.

The settlor, in creating a trust, can state the necessary provisions with respect to the duties and powers of the trustee and the rights of the beneficiaries; unless these provisions are contrary to any local policy or law, they are valid and enforceable. Most of the legal principles and rules governing trusts are applicable if the settlor does not provide otherwise.

Trusts are classified according to the manner of their creation as either made during the settlor's lifetime (*inter vivos*) or upon his or her death by a will (*testamentary*). An inter vivos, or living, trust is administered by the trustee, not only during the lifetime of the settlor but usually also after his or her death. A testamentary trust takes effect only upon death.

An *inter vivos* trust may be either revocable or irrevocable. The revocable *inter vivos* trust is one wherein the settlor reserves the power to terminate the trust at any time during his or her lifetime or to otherwise change its terms. Therefore, the settlor has the ability to cancel the trust completely or to change the disposition of either the principal or income or both as circumstances change during his or her lifetime. This revocability makes the property includable in his or her estate because of the retained power.

An irrevocable trust cannot be revoked and usually cannot be changed or modified. This restriction means that no beneficiaries may be added.

One of the basic purposes of estate planning is to pass the benefits of accumulated wealth from one individual to another in a manner that is in the best interests of the estate owner and that results in a minimal reduction of that wealth from taxes. The trust instrument is a valuable tool in estate planning, primarily because it permits considerable flexibility in the disposition and administration of property. The trust device not only saves taxes but also provides the flexibility needed to achieve many of the nontax objectives. Often other factors are just as important as effecting tax savings, such as prudent management of assets and the ability to give a trustee the right to use discretion as to the amount and timing of income and principal distributions.

Trusts may be classified in many different ways: by purpose, by manner of creation, or by status as revocable or irrevocable. A trust may be created to achieve any desired objective, as long as the objective is not illegal or contrary to any public policy or rule of law. Some of the more common types, classified by purpose, include insurance trusts, support trusts, charitable trusts, and marital deduction trusts.

Charitable trusts are originated in an effort to make one or more gifts to a charitable organization. In practice, charitable trusts generally are of two types. In the first type, a *charitable remainder trust*, the charity is to receive the remainder interest of the trust after some noncharitable beneficiary has received the income from the trust for some period of time.

In the second type of arrangement, called a *charitable lead trust* or a *charitable income trust*, the charity receives the income for a period, of years, with the remainder returning to the grantor or some other designated beneficiary.

A trust that is designed to provide support for a beneficiary is called a *support trust*. A support trust may provide for the continued administration of the trust property upon the incompetency or disability of the settlor. For example, the trust may provide for the income and principal of the trust to be given to family members during the incompetency of the settlor. This technique might avoid the establishment of a guardianship administration and the expenses associated with such a proceeding.

A living trust is set up during your life but becomes irrevocable upon death to assume ownership of your assets and to manage them according to your wishes. Those assets placed in the living trust do escape probate, but the assets do not escape the federal estate tax. Wills become public documents when probated, but the terms of a living will are not made public. Thus, although the assets do not get into the probate estate, the assets do get into taxable estate and may be taxable by the federal estate tax (see Key 28).

Large gifts may be made to children through the Uniform Gift to Minors Act or Uniform Transfers to Minors Act. Under a bank's or broker's account the gift does not incur the cost of setting up a trust. However, when the child reaches the age of legal majority (as low as 18 in some states), the account proceeds are distributed to the child.

32

TAX PLANNING

Few people can avoid confronting the income tax, whether as individuals paying for government services or as businesspeople concerned with a significant expense in the enterprise. You should pay what is legally due but not a dollar more, and it is likely that your payment can be reduced if you plan and organize. Actually tax-saved dollars are the best type of income: They're not taxable. Planning purposefully and keeping records effectively (see Key 9) will help you in nontax ways also.

Self-assessment means that you must determine, under the tax law, whether you are obligated to file a tax return and pay a tax. If so, it becomes your responsibility to file the tax return on your own initiative and to comply with the law regarding payment. But self-assessment applies primarily to the first step. After that, the system of enforcement demands compliance.

There is nothing wrong with trying to pay as little tax as possible—legally of course. Tax avoidance is fine, but tax evasion can result in free room and board in the Leavenworth Federal Prison. There is a fine line between tax avoidance and tax evasion—somewhat like the difference between lightning and a lightning bug. You may carefully save all of your deductible receipts to increase your itemized deductions, but you should not omit taxable income from your tax return.

The IRS does not punish tax offenders with public floggings as did the ancient Egyptian bureaucrats. However, there is an array of civil and criminal penalties to encourage you to pay your share of federal taxes.

With the right to assess interest on any amount due, and with more than 150 penalties available for it to impose, the IRS is a formidable adversary. In *A Law Unto Itself*, David Burnham describes the IRS as "the single most powerful instrument of social control in the country." To improve yourself economically, you need to have a working knowledge of the tax laws. Pay your taxes. Don't be a Pete Rose, Leona Helmsley, Willie Nelson, or Al Capone.

In nearly all tax disputes, the burden of proof is on the taxpayer. In a way, this means you essentially are guilty until proven innocent. So pay your federal taxes. In 1913 Representative Cordell Hull said that "every citizen should be willing to devote a brief time during some one day in the year, when necessary, to the making up of a listing of his income for taxes." It has been a long time since a "brief time" is sufficient to prepare the average tax return.

Recordkeeping is essential for compliance with tax laws. The likelihood of a happy outcome at a possible future audit is usually determined before the return is filed. An audit allows you to show the IRS that you are a good bookkeeper. Besides, organization and preparation can reduce taxes. Most taxpayers spend approximately a third of their working hours earning enough money to pay taxes. Remember, the best type of income is tax-saved dollars—those are not taxable.

All taxpayers must file a tax return each year and maintain accounting records to gather data for a current return. Accounting records include the taxpayer's regular books of account and such records and data as may be necessary to support entries on the tax return. The law does not specify the type of records a taxpayer should maintain, so they need not be elaborate or formal. A simple system should encourage prompt entries as income is received and payments for deductible expenses are made.

A taxpayer whose sole source of income is wages

need not keep formal accounting books. Copies of tax returns or other records may be sufficient to establish the method used to prepare income tax returns.

Failure to keep adequate records may increase your tax liability and also can get you penalized. The Tax Court has sustained a negligence penalty against a taxpayer who claimed certain business deductions but did not have the necessary documents to back them up. The taxpayer had maintained only a partial log for business expenses, and the court decided that some of the claimed expenses were "questionable."

At a minimum, tax returns and most records should be maintained for seven years. Previous tax returns can greatly simplify preparation of a current return. Sales slips, bills, invoices, receipts, canceled checks, and other documents often are sufficient to support tax deductions. Dates of sales and purchases of real estate and other investments can be important because of long-term and short-term calculations. Some records should be kept longer than seven years, including those involving home purchase and home improvement expenditures, retirement plan contributions, and receipts for assets that you are depreciating. Keep indefinitely the records that prove the tax basis of any assets that you hold (such as your home, securities, real estate). Keep copies of completed tax returns in a safe place. Taking time to accumulate, record, summarize, and retain the appropriate tax information can help reduce your taxes and increase your personal wealth. There are many home finance software packages that will interface with tax preparation software. This may be a good way for some people to track expenses, keep a budget, and maintain tax information.

Also remember that tax laws change. Whenever this happens, go over the changes to see how they affect your situation and your plans for the future.

A good source of information is the IRS web site at *www.irs.gov*. This site also has phone numbers for the

IRS offices and services in your state. If you want to speak with someone, order forms, or need an address, this web site has all of the contact information listed by state and for people living abroad.

Do not believe that dealing only in cash will hide income from the IRS. IRS agents can use the so-called net worth method to catch taxpayers who are hiding income by determining if they are living beyond their means. By comparing a person's net worth at the beginning and end of a year, an IRS agent can determine your increase or decrease in net worth. By subtracting funds from known sources (wages, dividends), funds from unknown or illegal sources can be determined.

For more information see Barron's *Keys to Saving Money on Income Tax* by Warren Boroson and *Keys to Surviving a Tax Audit* by D. Larry Crumbley and Jack Friedman.

33

PROPERTY TITLE AND JOINTLY HELD PROPERTY

There are several ways to own property: fee simple, tenancy in common, joint tenancy with rights of ownership, and community property.

Fee simple ownership means outright ownership by yourself. A fee simple owner is a sole and absolute owner. If you die, fee simple property is included in your gross estate at its fair market value on the date of your death.

There are various types of joint ownership of property. A tenancy in common is an undivided interest that can be transferred during life or death. In other words, to own property in tenancy in common is to own it with one or more other people. For example, you may own a duplex with another person, each of you owning half. You can sell your half during your lifetime. At death, the applicable portion of the undivided interest is included in your gross estate (that is, one half of the duplex).

In a joint tenancy with rights of survivorship, you own all of the property with someone else. You can give your interest away, or you can sell it. At death the property automatically passes to the surviving tenant.

The tax rules for property held jointly by spouses with survivorship rights are fairly simple. Each spouse is treated as one-half owner of joint tenancy assets, regardless of which spouse furnished the funds to acquire the property, and regardless of how the joint tenancy was created. Thus, when the first spouse dies, one half of the joint tenancy is included in gross estate, and only one half of any separate property will receive a *step-up in basis*. Step-up in basis is the difference between the price the decedent originally paid for an asset and its fair market value when an heir receives it. (Step-up basis for assets owned upon one's death is scheduled to disappear for decedents dying after 2009.) If an asset's value has increased, the resulting gain to the heir is not taxable to the heir, either when he or she receives the asset or when he or she eventually disposes of it. This step-up is an extremely important concept in financial planning.

For example, suppose a married couple owns land worth $190,000 for which they paid $40,000 many years ago in a separate-property state. The husband dies in 2002, and one half of the value of the land is included in his gross estate, but the appreciated value of the husband's half of the land is not taxed because of the unlimited marital deduction. The wife receives the land under the will with a basis stepped up to $115,000 ($40,000 + ($150,000/2)).

Assume instead that the husband owns the land outright and dies first. He could leave the land to his wife and obtain a marital deduction for the will transfer, paying no estate taxes. In this case, the wife receives a full step-up in basis to $190,000.

If the wife in the first example sells the land, she would have a $75,000 potential taxable gain, but the wife in the second example would have none. As these two examples demonstrate, joint ownership of property by married couples may no longer be appropriate because of the unlimited marital deduction.

States may be either common-law states or community property states. The ten community property law states are Arizona, California, Idaho, Louisiana, Nevada, New Mexico, Texas, Washington, Wisconsin, and Alaska (if elected by the spouses). All other states are classified as common-law states.

A person's state of residence determines how property is to be treated at the time it is acquired. In general, only property acquired during a marriage is community property. In community property states, any property acquired by spouses during marriage is construed to be one total community of property (spouses are considered 50-50 partners).

For tax purposes, only one half of the community property is included in the gross estate. Jointly held property in a community property state will include a full step-up in basis, including the surviving spouse's one-half interest in the community property. Thus, joint ownership in a community property state in order to avoid probate is still satisfactory.

For example, Bill Raby owns land in Texas (a community property state) jointly with rights of survivorship with his wife, Mary. Bill paid $70,000 for their land. At Bill's death in 2002, the land is valued at $230,000. Mary later sells the land for $240,000 and remarries. Mary would receive a full nontaxable step-up in basis to $230,000. However, the $10,000 difference between market value at Bill's death and the price she eventually receives for the land would be considered potential taxable gain.

34

TAX AND EDUCATION PLANNING FOR MINORS

Tax shelters may be defined as any operation that reduces taxes on current earnings. Tax laws allow many taxpayers to save money by using child-related tax shelters. Many Americans have used a process known as *income shifting* to shelter income from taxes. This technique focuses on shifting income from one family member (the parent) to another (the child), who is in a lower tax bracket. This income-shifting strategy is still available under current tax law but to a much lesser extent than in years past.

One important provision under current tax law concerns who gets to claim the personal exemption for a child who is working part time. Under present law, children who are claimed as dependents on their parents' tax return cannot claim the personal exemption on their own tax return. Current law requires parents to provide a Social Security number (except in special circumstances) for each child claimed as a dependent. One purpose of this requirement is to eliminate the potential for use of fictitious names by parents attempting to secure a larger exemption.

Under a current tax provision called a "kiddie tax" on investment income, earnings in excess of $1,500 from savings or other investments held by a child under age 14 are taxed at his or her custodial parents' marginal tax rate. As a result, parents are unable to shelter large amounts of income by putting their investments in their children's name in an attempt to avoid taxes.

Current tax law permits fewer income-shifting techniques than existed previously. A dependent who has unearned income in excess of a designated amount ($750 in 2002) must file a tax return. (For current information, check the IRS web site, *www.irs.ustreas.gov.*) As a result, more parents must file tax returns for their children. The IRS provides an alternative to filing a tax return for a child by allowing parents to report the child's income on their return by filing Form 8814. Moreover, under current law, a parent to whom the kiddie tax applies must provide the parent's taxpayer identification number for inclusion on the child's return. Failure to do so may subject the parent to penalties.

Earned income is any amount received as pay for work done. A child's unearned income includes unearned income attributable to property transferred to the child, gifts from persons other than parents, and gifts made under the Uniform Gifts to Minors Act. It also includes unearned income derived from the child's earned income, such as interest on bank deposits.

The following rules apply to the taxation of children under the age of 14. The first $750 of the child's unearned income is not taxed at all since this amount is regarded as the child's standard deduction. The next $750 is taxed at the child's tax rate. Any earnings in excess of $1,500 will be taxed at the parents' marginal tax rate (their top tax rate). These amounts may change from year to year (adjusted for inflation). For current amounts, check the IRS web site (*www.irs.ustreas.gov*).

If you have children, you should consider taking advantage of the $750 standard deduction. This deduction can save taxes on $750 of any type of income.

Considering the spread between the lowest and highest marginal tax rate (15 to 38.6 percent in 2002; tax rates will be gradually reduced to range from 10 percent to 33 percent in 2006), people in high tax brackets should consider making gifts to relatives, especially children over age 13 (to avoid the kiddie tax). A single person can give up to $11,000 ($22,000 for a married couple) per year, per donee, without incurring a gift tax.

There are several investment and tax-saving strategies available to parents. Depending on the specific rules for a given type of investment, parents may be able to maximize a child's income and minimize the related tax liability. The investments suggested here often serve as a means of deferring income until the child reaches the age of 14 when he or she will be able to avoid the kiddie tax.

U.S. savings bonds can be an effective part of a tax-saving strategy involving children. The Series EE bond is one of the most popular of the U.S. savings bonds, and it is also one of the most practical investments. These bonds may be purchased at half of their face value.

Minors may defer income on Series EE bonds until the bonds are redeemed or until the child elects to recognize the income. On the date of maturity or redemption, the child collects the face value of the bond plus additional interest if rates have increased. Interest is calculated by subtracting the price paid for the bond from the amount received on redemption. If bonds are redeemed prior to maturity, interest is based on the initial rate established when the bonds were purchased. This means that bonds redeemed prior to maturity will *not* earn additional interest *even if* rates have increased since the bonds were purchased. Therefore, deferring the interest until maturity seems to be the most profitable alternative. If you defer reporting the interest on the Series EE bonds, you can effectively shift the taxation of this interest income to your children. If the bonds are purchased under the child's name and do not mature or are not sold until after the child reaches 14 years of age, interest income will be taxed at the child's lower rate.

An additional tax-saving technique using Series EE bonds is for parents to buy the bonds and use the proceeds at maturity to pay for a child's college tuition. In such cases, the interest income on the bonds is exempt from federal income tax. This benefit, however, is phased out under current tax law for single taxpayers with income over $69,100, and for joint taxpayers with AGI over $111,100.

There are a few other restrictions in order to get the education expense exemption. First, you must be at least 24 years old on the day you purchase the bonds. You do not need to specify that you intend to use them for education when you buy them. You must, however, use the proceeds of the bonds for qualified educational expenses in the same calendar year that they are redeemed. If the educational expenses are for your child, the bonds must be in your name or your spouse's name. You can list your child as the beneficiary of the bond, but your child cannot be a co-owner if you want the tax-free interest. If the expenses are to be used for your own education, then the bonds must be in your name and you must file a joint tax return if you are married. In addition to series EE bonds, Series I bonds can also be used in this way. Additional information about these and other types of savings bonds can be found at *www.savingsbonds.gov.*

Life insurance is another way of deferring income until a child reaches age 14 (see Key 13). Money placed into life insurance policies accumulates interest on a tax-deferred basis until the funds are withdrawn. Your child will then pay taxes on the difference between the premium and the amount that is withdrawn. Because of the tax-free interest, many universal and whole life policies are being pushed as a means for parents to accumulate money for their children's college. An example furnished by Metropolitan Life demonstrates that $10,000 invested at 8.75 percent grows to $45,261 after 18 years.

Gifts of growth stocks and appreciating property under the Uniform Gifts to Minors Act provide parents with an effective tool for transferring property to a child under the age of 14. This technique provides parents with another means for delaying the taxation of income.

Transferring stock or property to a child enables you to avoid any tax consequences until the stock or property is sold. Upon the sale of the property after the child turns 14, tax is imposed only on capital gains, which are taxed at the child's presumably lower rate.

Stocks of companies with low dividend payout rates and high growth potential are the best choice for shifting income in this way. The obvious risk with this type of investment is that the stock's value might decline rather than increase.

Transfers of appreciating property are more complicated than transfers of growth stocks. There are two forms of property transfers: absolute and partial. In an absolute transfer, the transferor gives the title and interest to the child forever. In a partial transfer, the transferor gives up title and interest to the property for a specified period of time.

Employing a child in the family business benefits the parent not only because of the services rendered but also because of the business deduction generated by the wages. The money the child earns as an employee is not subject to kiddie tax treatment because it is earned income.

A child's wage income is considered ordinary income, and is therefore subject to the $4,700 (in 2002) standard deduction. This means that the first $4,700 a child earns is not taxed. Hiring a child for a legitimate job in a family business can save taxes two ways. First, the parent can deduct the wages from the taxable income of the business, and second, the child owes no taxes on his or her earnings up to the amount of the standard deduction.

If the parent cannot claim the child as a dependent, then the child may claim the personal exemption on his or her tax return. However, since most parents do supply over half of their child's support, they must claim the child as a dependent on their return.

Salaries, wages, and other compensation paid to children are a deductible business expense as long as the compensation: (1) is an ordinary and necessary business expense, (2) is reasonable in amount, (3) is based on actual services rendered, and (4) is actually paid or incurred.

What constitutes ordinary and necessary expense? Only those taxpayers engaged in a trade or business may deduct as a business expense wages paid to their children for work performed in connection with that business. Payments for performing odd jobs around the house do *not* qualify as a business expense. A child must be hired to do something that the parent would be willing to hire another person to do.

What constitutes reasonable compensation? Compensation to children is considered reasonable if the parent would pay another nonfamily member the same amount for the work performed. Reasonable compensation is an important issue in the employment of children. The Internal Revenue Service looks carefully at payments made to relatives. Proper documentation and record-keeping are essential (see Key 9). The parents must maintain records for children just as they would for any other employee. If you are audited, the burden of proof is on the parent.

There have been several cases in which the Internal Revenue Service has stepped in and questioned "reasonable compensation." For example, in one case, a physician employed his child, who was under 12 years of age. He paid the child $11,000 for helping in his office and performing duties that included trash emptying, mail sorting, and answering telephones. The court found it hard to believe that an intelligent and educated professional would pay $11,000 for office services performed by a small child on a part-time basis. The court held, accordingly, that the wages were not reasonable for the services performed and therefore were not deductible. If the facts and circumstances do not support the taxpayer's position, the IRS can recharacterize the payment as a taxable gift or dividend income and deny tax deductions for amounts exceeding reasonable compensation.

A family partnership is another potentially useful tool for shifting income and appreciation of capital assets to younger-generation family members. In a family partnership, the parents relinquish part of their ownership in a business to their children. Family partnerships are complicated, and their success depends on the type of business and how the child contributes to the business operations. Making a child a partner in name only is ineffective in reducing tax liability. The child must have an actual ownership in the partnership. Parents should carefully weigh the benefits and the costs associated with creating a family partnership. Setting up such partnerships can be very costly. If the child is a minor, the parent may be required to hire someone to act as a partner in the child's behalf.

If parents are in a position to employ children, that option should be strongly considered. A child benefits from the extra money that he or she makes, and the parents can benefit from the services performed while deducting the child's wages from their business income.

Saving for a college education is a huge task. This task can be made much simpler if the appropriate planning is done when children are young. There are many options available to help save for college. In addition, if your children are older, there are other ways to pay for these expenses.

If you have the advantage of having small children or are considering starting a family soon, this is the right time to start thinking about your child's college education. The first step will be to determine how much of your child's education you will fund, if any, and how you will fund this amount in the coming years.

One way to do this is to purchase Series EE or I savings bonds. Both I bonds and EE bonds can be purchased at banks, credit unions, through payroll deductions, or through regular savings account deductions.

Regular deductions to purchase bonds may be a good way to systematically save for your child's or for your education.

An Education IRA is another way to save for college. An IRA account may be set up for any child under age 18 and may have contributions made by parents, other family members, friends, and the child himself up to a total of $2,000 per year (lifetime maximum of $36,000—18 years at $2,000 per year). The amounts will grow tax-free until they are withdrawn and will remain tax-free if the amounts are used for qualified education expenses, such as tuition, fees, and books. If the child does not need the amounts for post-secondary education, they can be rolled over to the education IRA of certain other family members.

A 529 plan is a college savings plan under section 529 of the Internal Revenue Code. A 529 plan can be either a prepaid tuition plan or a college savings plan that is administered through state governments. States may have slightly different rules and may offer other tax savings for state income tax. You do not necessarily have to reside in a state to set up a plan in that state. The prepaid tuition plan will be discussed later, so the savings plan will be discussed here. The savings plan allows contributions to grow tax-free for as long as they are in the plan and beginning in 2002, withdrawals are tax-exempt if they are used for qualified higher education costs. The advantages of this plan are that the funds are professionally managed, there are no age or income limits, and the owner of the account maintains control over the funds. The contributions are treated as gifts to the beneficiary and qualify for the $10,000 gift tax exclusion. In addition, contribution limits are high compared to other college savings plans (more than $200,000 may be maintained in this type of plan). There may also be advantages to the 529 savings plan over the prepaid plan. The prepaid plan may affect financial aid status of your child, while the savings plan is considered an asset of the parent and only a portion of this reduces the amount of financial aid offered. Another advantage is that the savings plan may be set up for any beneficiary including the owner of the plan.

Prepaid tuition plans allow parents to lock in today's college tuition prices. The plans will vary by state, but can be purchased as soon as a child is born and financed for a set number of years or for older children during the number of years until matriculation to college. If your child does not go to college, the amount paid in is refunded less administrative fees. Interest accrued will be paid according to the rules for that state's plan. This is one way to avoid the steep increase in college fees and to save for college over a number of years. The great thing about these types of funds is that they are guaranteed by the state and no matter how much tuition and fees increase or how much volatility there is in the stock market the price of tuition is locked in at the time you join the plan. An Internet search for "prepaid tuition" or "529 Plans" can help you find if your state offers either or both of these types of plans.

If you have older children and do not have as much time to save for college, there are other ways to finance your child's education. You may want to consider having your child attend a junior college for some of the basic courses and then transfer to a four-year institution for the last two years. This is a good way to save costs on tuition. In addition, there may be a junior college close to home that will help save on housing expenses.

Other options for paying for college expenses include applying for federal financial aid such as Perkins loans and Pell Grants. Some universities will offer low-interest loans to students or their parents as part of a financial aid packages. You should also look into scholarship and grant opportunities. There are many scholarships available for a variety of talents (such as a music scholarship). In addition, some scholarships may be available based on your or your child's background, residence, or social activities. Keep in mind that sometimes the restrictions on scholarships, such as the requirement that the child must be a resident of a certain community or have been a Girl Scout, can limit the competition. Your child may have a good shot at the scholarship even if he or she does not have a 4.0 GPA since many children will be excluded because they are not from that neighborhood or because they were not Girl Scouts. Researching scholarships and completing applications and essays can be time consuming, however the payoff may be great. Look for opportunities once your child has started college as well. Many times there are departmental scholarships or university scholarships for students who have a specific educational interest or who have contributed to the college in some way.

Work-study programs are also available at most schools. Students may be able to work a limited number of hours per week at the college and earn a wage to be used for school and living expenses. Many college students work 10 to 20 hours per week; jobs include working in the library, the student recreation center, or for an academic department in the school. Another possibility related to work-study is internship programs. These programs are usually available to students once they are upperclassmen. The student will leave school for a semester and work for a company that is related to the field that they are studying. For example, a computer science major may intern with a company like IBM. During this time the student earns a salary similar to one earned by a new employee for the 3–4-month period that they are employed. This money can then be used to help cover expenses at school. Some students may choose to complete more than one internship in order to gain job experience and earn more money. Internship information can usually be obtained at the college's career services department.

35

SURVIVING AN IRS AUDIT

Once a taxpayer submits a return to the IRS, it goes through an IRS computer that checks for mathematical accuracy and completeness. The IRS uses a computerized program to match third-party information returns (W-2s, 1099s), such as for wages, interest, dividends, and certain deductions, with the amounts reported on the tax returns. Computers also process this information to identify taxpayers who have received income but have not filed tax returns. When third-party information returns do not agree with a filed tax return, the taxpayer is sent a letter that asks for an explanation of the discrepancy.

Computers also check to see whether other items, such as deductions, interest, dividend income, and capital gains, fall within normal ranges. The Discriminant Function Formula (DFF) picks tax returns that are likely to contain errors, cheating, or understatement of taxes.

The audit procedure starts when you get a letter from the IRS informing you that your tax return is to be examined and specifying whether the examination is an office or field audit. Don't let the letter scare you. Just get prepared.

Two comments. First, never give original records to an agent or to an IRS office, instead, give copies. If you give original documentation, you run the risk of losing it. Second, if a "special agent" is conducting the audit, the IRS may suspect fraud, and you would be well advised to obtain a lawyer immediately. Also, if you hear of an IRS agent checking with your bank or stock-broker or asking your neighbor questions about you, get a lawyer and take your records from your accountant or any other nonlawyer tax adviser. Communication with a nonlawyer is not considered privileged.

Being audited is not a pleasant experience, but neither is it an accusation of wrongdoing. As defined by the IRS, an audit is an impartial review of a tax return to determine its accuracy and completeness. There are three main types of audits:

1. Correspondence
2. Office
3. Field

At the various IRS service centers, tax returns are reviewed for obvious errors such as overstated standard deductions, incorrect tax calculation, and incorrect filing status (for example, improperly claiming to be a head of household). The taxpayer receives a computer-printed letter proposing a correction in the tax. If a taxpayer's return is selected for examination and the return is relatively simple or a minor point is in question, a correspondence audit may occur. The IRS writes to the taxpayer to request information. Once the IRS is satisfied, the issue is settled.

A tax return may be selected for an office audit. In this case, the taxpayer is asked to present tax records and supporting information to the director's office at a prescribed date and time. A taxpayer has a number of rights during this process. Many office audits are begun and completed in a single session. If agreement is not reached with the examining officer, the taxpayer has the right to confer with an appeals office to see if a settlement can be worked out. A written request will get a conference in an office audit case.

If a tax return is relatively complicated—if it includes business operations, many types of income, or intricate financial transactions, for example—the IRS examination will be conducted as a field audit. This means that the IRS agent conducts the examination at your office, place of business, home, or representative's office. Aside from this difference in venue, the procedure is generally the same as for an office audit.

After a tax return has been examined, a refund is allowed, a deficiency is proposed, a no-change report is filed, or a "partial" is issued. A "partial" is an agreement whereby the taxpayer accedes to some of the issues and proposed adjustments but not all. In the case of a deficiency, if no agreement is reached with the examining agent on the amount, the agent writes what is called a Revenue Agent's Report (RAR). The agent submits the report to his or her group manager, who in turn submits it to the review staff. The case then goes to the 30-day unit, which sends a 30-day letter. If no protest is filed, a Statutory Notice of Deficiency (90-day letter) is sent.

IRS personnel are human. Like you, they are under great stress; they must deal with rude taxpayers, arrogant tax practitioners, and an unyielding bureaucracy. Given this high-pressure environment, it is best to avoid acrimony in dealing with them. It is in your best interest to be courteous, respectful, cheerful, and cooperative.

During an audit interview, answer only the questions asked. You may save a lot of time and anxiety if you can get the auditor to state at the outset what he or she is looking for. Answer questions truthfully—but you need not tell everything. There is a fine line between providing enough information and providing too much. Think of the auditor as a fact finder, but don't suggest new areas of inquiry.

Allow the auditor to look at your documents and records only once. In a field audit, do not allow the auditor to have access to a copy machine or to take original documents away from your premises. Make copies of documents that the auditor requests and provide these.

Do not complain about the tax system. IRS people have to pay taxes also, and they see a lot of people who are not paying their share. You should appear to be willing to pay the taxes you owe, but no more. Never appear to be a tax protester.

Keep in mind that an auditor is examining you and your lifestyle as well as your tax return. Therefore, your appearance should not call attention to itself. For example, it may be a good idea to forego wearing your Rolex watch or mink coat to the audit.

In an office or field audit, you are instructed to bring specific records. Have those records organized in a logical fashion. If your records indicate a businesslike approach to record-keeping, your audit may be brief. Summary sheets that are backed up by receipts improve your chances of receiving a no-change audit report. An auditor who has to spend time sorting out your records is more likely to disallow the item in question and may even uncover new problems.

36

ANNUITY AND LEVERAGING CONCEPTS

One way to help accumulate wealth is to adopt the annuity concept in your daily life. An annuity is an amount payable annually or at other regular intervals, such as monthly, quarterly, or semiannually, for the duration of the lives of one or more beneficiaries, including payments for a specified term after the death of an annuitant.

Most such contracts are issued by life insurance companies and are issued either as an annuity policy purchased as such or as an optional mode of settlement under a life insurance policy or an endowment policy. In purchases of annuity policies from insurance companies, the premium can consist of only one payment of cash (single premium) or of annual payments. When a life insurance policy matures on the death of an insured, the beneficiary, instead of taking the proceeds in a lump sum, is typically offered a number of options, one being the right to receive an annuity for life. Similarly, on the maturity of an endowment policy, the owner is usually permitted to elect payment in the form of an annuity.

To use the annuity concept of financial planning, look for ways where a small amount of effort will result in revenue over a number of years. Income from book royalties, song royalties, patent royalties, computer software royalties, and television and commercial royalties fall within this criteria. Some large sweepstake winners or lottery winners are paid by the annuity method.

For example, you may moonlight as a writer. You

subscribe to *Writer's Digest* and earn some money from writing articles for magazines. You then write a self-help book, and you receive royalties of 5 to 15 percent from each book sold. The more books sold, the more income you receive. Write books that sell over several years, such as books for universities, colleges, or high schools that will be used year after year. Movie scripts can also generate cash for years. Some scripts for movies sold for $1 million in the early nineties.

Royalty income from an invention also illustrates the annuity concept. Imagine the royalty income to the inventors of the paper clip, the stick-on yellow pad, the flea collar, or the fax machine.

A patent is a nonrenewable right, granted by various governments, that enables the recipient to exclude others from the manufacture, sale, or other use of an invention for a period of 17 years from the date of the grant. If you have a patent for a product that continues to sell well, you could receive royalty payments over a 17-year period.

A license agreement can be similar to a royalty agreement. You agree to allow someone else to use patented, copyrighted, or proprietary (trade secrets) material in return for a royalty payment. The key is that someone else is using your idea, and they are paying you year after year. But if you grant an exclusive license, you, the licensor, will be excluded from marketing the invention.

Why not invent a trade secret or secret recipe? The best example is the Coca-Cola formula. It all began with an Atlanta pharmacist, John S. Pembeton, who registered a trademark for French Wine Cola—"ideal nerve and tonic stimulant." His first advertisement appeared in May 1886, but he sold too soon. He granted all rights to Coke to Asa Candler, an Atlanta businessman, for $2,300 in 1891. In 1919 the company was sold for $25 million. That's a return of about 10,870 percent in 28 years (or 388 percent per year).

Customer and supplier lists can be very valuable to

certain businesses and provide another way of generating income repeatedly from one source. If you have a way of obtaining names of suppliers or customers, and if you have authorization, you can sell these names to other businesses.

A franchise also utilizes this annuity concept of having money paid to you year after year (for example, Subway, McDonalds).

Another way to accumulate wealth is through the technique of leveraging, or using borrowed money. Leveraging became one of the most frequently heard buzzwords during the 1980s and is associated with some of the most financially profitable ventures as well as the worst financial failures of the decade. Much of the savings and loans disaster of the late 1980s was caused by people and businesses trying to leverage.

Leveraging is a two-edged sword. The multiplier effect of leveraging can generate either high levels of income or crippling debt, depending upon the success of the individual or business. Commodity traders, for example, take advantage of leveraging. They buy a commodity on margin and put a small amount of principal down. If the price of the commodity goes up, they multiply their income. But if the price goes south, they multiply their losses.

Technically, leveraging may be defined as the use of supplementary nonequity capital to increase your return on equity (your net worth). In a business, leveraging tends to magnify the effect on earnings per share of an increase or decrease in dollar sales. But when you leverage, *you assume risk*. If earnings fail to meet projections, you may have trouble meeting payments on your debt.

Leveraging can be used in your personal life. You may not have enough savings to purchase an automobile with cash, so you leverage by buying on credit. Since the tax laws no longer allow a deduction for personal interest payments, it is more difficult for individuals to use the tax laws to benefit from leveraging.

You can use leveraging when you assume a mortgage on your home. The property is purchased with a small down payment, and the interest expense and real estate taxes are deductible on the tax return (see Key 21).

Refinancing your home via a second mortgage or so-called home equity loan is another form of leveraging that permits you to realize tax-free cash, increase cash flows from the property, or reduce interest costs. If you have a large amount of consumer debt (perhaps from credit cards), the interest you pay on such debt is not deductible. You may wish to refinance your home *and* pay off the high-interest consumer debt. Your mortgage interest expense may be deductible.

Leveraging is an important factor in rental real estate. Mortgage financing has two major virtues. First, when rental or business property is purchased, its basis for depreciation purposes is not limited to the cash or equity investment. The depreciable basis includes the money borrowed to finance the acquisition. Since your total depreciation deduction may exceed any cash investment, this shelters income from taxation.

The second major advantage of mortgage financing is that you aren't taxed on funds that you borrow. Thus, you may purchase part of your real estate investment tax free by simply borrowing against the property.

37

REAL ESTATE INVESTING

Of all investments that provide tax incentives, real estate is the most often used. Frequently, books and articles for the general public appear that feature titles such as "How to Make a Fortune in Real Estate" or "Real Estate Investments Can Make You Independently Wealthy." Any late night and early morning you can watch a television show encouraging you to "make a fortune in real estate."

The way to make a profit in real estate investments has changed considerably during the last decade. There have been major changes in tax laws as well as in the economic environment. Rental property investments have lost some of their tax shelter features. When the top marginal tax rate was reduced in 1986, the advantage of the rental property tax loss became correspondingly less. Another major tax shelter feature, the rapid write-off of the investment via accelerated depreciation, was replaced by a longer, straight-line depreciation method. However, the reduction in the capital gain rates has improved the tax advantage of real estate. Clearly, as a tax shelter, rental property is somewhat less attractive now than in previous years due to modest inflation, leaner write-offs, and modest rises in real estate prices. But with the new 38.6 percent individual rate starting July 1, 2001 through 2003, the spread between the highest rate and the maximum capital gain rate of 20 percent is now 18.6 percent. The overall drop in real estate values in some areas has provided an opportunity to purchase undeveloped land, residential rental property, and commercial property at low prices.

Inflation generally creates disincentives for capital investment because of tax regulations that do not permit adjustments for inflation. For example, assume that the tax rate is applied to the difference between cash receipts (for example, income to a cash-basis taxpayer) and depreciation. Since the law does not permit the depreciation deduction to increase with inflation, depreciation stays constant while cash receipts increase. Thus, the sum that is taxed grows larger and real taxes paid grow larger. Cash flow is cash receipts minus tax; thus real cash flow grows smaller. As long as depreciation is not adjusted, real cash flow will decrease as inflation accelerates.

Even though there is a negative impact of inflation (when combined with taxes) on real cash flow of capital investments, there may be some offsetting positive factors for investments in rental property. One positive factor provided by the federal government is a tax deduction for depreciation. A second positive factor is that rental property investments may appreciate in value, thus providing a nontaxable return on investment (until sold).

1. One advantage of an investment in rental property is that it generates a cash flow in the form of rental payments to the property owner. The cash flow is usually steady and reliable, depending, of course, on the lessee. The lease contract or rental agreement normally specifies the amount and time of payments.
2. Since the supply of real estate is limited, it is expected that well-selected real estate will increase in value at least as fast as inflation reduces the value of the dollar. Thus, a second advantage of real estate investment is that it provides a hedge against inflation.

3. A third nontax advantage of real estate investments is that they may be obtained by using financial leverage (see Key 36). Financial leverage can be defined as the use of borrowed funds under the anticipation that the rate of increase in the value of the property will be greater than the cost of borrowing, therefore, the investor will realize a profit not only on his or her own money but also on the use of the creditor's money.
4. Real estate investments may create equity that can be used for other investments. Debt reduction, as well as inflation, may create equity that can be a source of new or additional financing. Equity accumulation is a fourth advantage of real estate investment.
5. A fifth advantage to individual investors is that many real estate investments can be obtained with nonrecourse mortgage debt (that is, the investor is not personally liable). Thus, the investor has limited liability.

There are disadvantages, of course. Real estate acquisition usually requires a substantial investment and longer holding periods than other types of investments. For example, to realize the full tax benefits of depreciation, the property must be held at least $27^1/_2$ years for residential rental real estate and 39 years for nonresidential real estate. On the other hand, an investor might purchase a few shares of stock without a financial strain and realize the tax benefits after holding the stock for a much shorter period.

Thus, two disadvantages of real estate investments are the *relatively large investment requirement* and the *longer holding period*. In addition, before buying real estate, the investor must carefully assess market value to determine if the purchase price of the property is reasonable. So a third disadvantage of real estate investment is the *problem of appraisal.*

A fourth major disadvantage is the *disallowance of passive losses*. By definition, real estate is a passive activity, and the passive loss rules generally disallow 100 percent of losses on real estate activities. In other words, losses from real estate activities may not be offset against your portfolio income (such as interest and dividends) or your active income (such as salary or business or consulting income).

There are major exceptions to the passive loss rules for rental real estate activities. A person with adjusted gross income (AGI) less than $100,000 may deduct up to $25,000 of passive losses against portfolio and nonpassive income. The person must actively participate in the rental real estate activity. This annual $25,000 deduction is reduced by 50 percent of your AGI in excess of $100,000, so that an individual with an AGI of $150,000 or larger has no deduction. Starting in 1994 a real estate professional may offset passive losses from real estate activities against all income sources. In general, the person must spend more than one half of his or her personal service in real estate and more than 750 hours per year in real estate activities.

A fifth disadvantage is *marketability*. The ability to sell real estate may vary greatly due to changes in the economy (recession or growth), supply and demand factors, and the cost of financing. Typically, there will be times when you will be unable to sell your real estate investment at what you consider a "fair" price.

Related to marketability is liquidity. An investor can realize cash from an investment in stock in a few days, but acquiring cash on a sale of real property may take a long time. Thus, a sixth disadvantage of real estate investments is *decreased liquidity*.

A seventh possible disadvantage is *high financing costs*. High financing costs make many investments marginal or uneconomic. A few years ago, the introduction of variable-interest-rate mortgage loans made this an area requiring careful analysis. Currently, mortgage interest rates are lower than they were a few years ago, and fixed-interest-rate loans are widely available. However, financing costs remain an important consideration in the investment decision process.

Last but not least important, real estate can be a nuisance and source of aggravation. If you manage the real estate, there will be midnight (and later) calls about broken air conditioners and heating systems, broken and frozen pipes, leaking roofs, broken doors, and lost keys. It takes a certain mentality to suffer this grief from tenants. A summary of these points is provided in Exhibit 37.1.

EXHIBIT 37.1
Summary of Advantages and Disadvantages of Real Estate Investing

Advantages	Disadvantages
1. Generates Cash Flow	1. Relatively Large Investment
2. Hedge Against Inflation	2. Requires Longer Holding Period
3. Can Use Financial Leverage to Buy	3. Appraisal of Value
4. Create Equity for Other Investments	4. Disallowance of Passive Losses
5. Can Obtain with Nonrecourse Debt	5. Marketability
	6. Decreased Liquidity
	7. High Financing Costs
	8. Management Can Be Aggravating

With all of these disadvantages, we do not wish to be too pessimistic because fortunes can still be made in real estate. Depreciation is an important factor in the tax economics of improved real estate. Few other forms of investment permit a deduction of a portion of the cost of the asset prior to sale. While depreciation is intended as a recovery of the cost of such property over its physical or economic life, in actuality a carefully maintained property (the cost of maintenance is also deductible) may decline in value at a rate less than that allowed for tax depreciation. Through inflation and increased land values, many strategically located properties will increase in value.

Other than direct ownership of raw land, residential property, and commercial property (which the authors prefer), there are several indirect ways of owning real estate.

REIT. A *real estate investment trust* (REIT) is like a mutual fund. You invest money in an REIT, and management buys apartment complexes, shopping centers, and other real estate. If the REIT pays out at least 90 percent of its taxable income to the shareholders, its income is not taxed like a corporation. In addition, a REIT is more liquid than direct investment in real estate. About one third of all REITs are listed on the New York and American Stock Exchanges.

A real estate limited partnership is organized by general partners who buy and manage properties. You, an investor called a *limited partner*, contribute money to the partnership and avoid the day-to-day hassles. In theory, you have limited liability, but be careful because many so-called limited partnerships may require you to contribute more investment capital, and they are extremely illiquid. Income and losses from a limited partnership are considered passive.

Choosing an investment is often difficult because of the many factors involved. There are numerous tax and nontax considerations that must be carefully evaluated before rental property is acquired. Some of these are as follows: cash flows, hedge against inflation, equity accumulation, large investment requirement, marketability, liquidity, high financing costs, and depreciation. Your financial position and investment objectives must be carefully evaluated in light of the aforementioned considerations.

One tax shelter left in real estate is the low-income

housing tax credit. If an investment is approved, low-income housing provides an investor an annual tax credit up to 9 percent of the value of any investment for ten years. In essence, you can recoup up to 90 percent of this investment over ten years through this tax break. The annual tax credit is limited to the amount of taxes you would owe on $25,000.

Generally, the project must remain active for 15 years and comply with low-income-housing standards; otherwise, the tax savings are subject to recapture. The primary tool for this shelter is the limited partnership. These partnership units are not liquid.

Another real estate tax shelter is the rehabilitation tax credit. There is a 20 percent tax credit for rehabilitating certified historic structures and a 10 percent credit for industrial and commercial property placed into service before 1936. Thus, if you were to rehabilitate a building for your business, you could take a tax credit of 10 or 20 percent of the costs of rehabilitation against your tax liability.

For more information see Barron's *Keys to Investing in Real Estate* by Jack C. Harris and Jack P. Friedman.

38

INTERNATIONALIZE YOURSELF

The world is becoming smaller. Changes have been swift. Tiananmen Square. Reunited Germany. Kuwait. Breakup of the former Soviet Union. The World Trade Center attack. You should think globally. Try to internationalize yourself. Travel as much as possible. Learn to speak a foreign language. Rather than reading *Newsweek, Time, or U.S. News & World Report*, subscribe to *The Economist*. Become an expert in several foreign countries.

Globalization is spawning many challenges and opportunities. Companies have been engaged in international business for thousands of years. Why does international business receive so much attention today? For one thing, there has been a dramatic increase in international operations over the last few years. International business issues are frequently making headlines, such as the U.S. trade deficit and the "Japanese style" of doing business. Eastern Europe is opening up. The Iron Curtain is down, and the former Soviet Union and China are "hot."

International operations are increasingly important to all types of business firms. Many multinational firms are either expanding international operations or are becoming part of other multinational firms via mergers or acquisitions. As a result, many firms are providing products and services to customers and clients around the globe. Companies must create marketing analyses that deal with geographical, linguistic, and cultural differences.

International trade is part of doing business for both large and small firms. Even a relatively small firm may have operations in foreign locations. The federal government has provided significant incentives to promote international operations, including laws providing for export trading companies and foreign sales corporations.

Not many years ago, the people involved in international activities were often committed to making the foreign country their homes for many years or even for the rest of their lives, and consequently had to learn the foreign languages. Today there is much less emphasis on learning other languages. However, there are indications that this situation is changing. After years of having no foreign language requirement, many universities are now requiring all entering students to have completed two years of a foreign language in high school or to complete two courses once they are admitted to the university. An article in *Fortune* magazine listed six priorities for American M.B.A. programs. The first was to give students a global perspective and to require knowledge of a foreign language and culture.

Many Americans are totally unprepared for adapting to foreign cultures. To compound the problem, the foreign work environment may operate under a different organization structure, with different policies and procedures. These factors now are taken into account by the multinational's human resources department as they consider candidates for overseas assignment.

Preparation is the key to a successful international assignment. Paul J. Quinn, Jr., an international manager with International Multifoods Corporation, urges Americans to work or travel abroad to familiarize themselves with the customs of foreign nations. Paul Salzinger, international sales and marketing director for Ashton-Tate, says that cultures, not languages, become a critical issue. He says that he constantly reminds people to be sensitive to other cultures.

Many business travelers today learn foreign languages to facilitate their trips abroad. A number of high-quality cassette courses are available, ranging in price from $20 to $200. Approximately 40 hours of listening, repeating, and reading are necessary for a person to master the basics.

International operations are increasingly important in today's global economy. Opportunities abound for persons willing to travel to foreign locations.

Investing in international stocks is an excellent way to diversify a stock portfolio. An investor can buy foreign stocks individually, but there are several other methods for investing in foreign stocks. The three most popular ways for individual investors are as follows: (1) mutual funds, (2) American Depository Receipts, and (3) iShares.

Mutual Funds. The easiest way to invest in foreign securities is to purchase shares in a mutual fund that invests in such securities. This course of action would be preferable for investors who lack the time or inclination to investigate foreign markets. International stock funds offer the advantage of participation in a diversified portfolio of foreign stocks in addition to professional management. International funds are available that specialize in particular regions, such as Asia, or specific countries, such as Mexico or Germany. Prior to purchasing any of these funds, a copy of the prospectus should be obtained, which describes the investment philosophy of the fund.

American Depository Receipts. Individuals who wish to purchase individual foreign securities should purchase American Depository Receipts (ADRs), which are negotiable investments representing ownership of stock in a foreign corporation traded on an exchange. ADRs are issued only on widely held and actively traded corporations. Further, they are liquid and have transaction costs comparable to U.S. stocks. At least 600 foreign companies are issued by an U.S. bank and represent shares on deposit with that bank's foreign office or custodian. ADRs allow investors to buy or sell foreign stocks without actually taking physical possession of the underlying securities. Purchase is made in U.S. dollars, and dividends are received in U.S. dollars. The best web sites for information and prices are *www.adr.com* and *www.bankofny.com.*

iShares. In 1996 the AMEX expanded its index offerings by launching WEBS (World Equity Bank Shares), which are designed to give investors fast and economical access to the international equity markets. In 2000 these indexes were renamed iShares, and some other market sectors added. Through a single security, investors can own a diversified foreign country stock portfolio that seeks to track the performance of a major benchmark index. Each iShare series represents an investment in a portfolio of publicly traded stocks in a selected country (for example, Japan, EWJ). Investment results are sought that correspond to the price and yield performance of a specific Morgan Stanley Capital International Index (MSCI). MSCI indexes are leading country index benchmarks widely used by U.S. investors for their international investments.

ETFs. Unlike American Depository Receipts (ADRs) that provide an investment in just one company, iShares offer targeted exposure to a portfolio of publicly traded foreign stocks in a selected country and certain market sectors. Currently, iShares embrace 22 country-specific series of securities (for example, Australia, EWA). The iShares are the most recently introduced example of exchange traded funds (ETFs).

ETFs are not mutual funds in the traditional sense; rather, they are hybrid instruments combining aspects of common stocks and mutual funds and offering many of the benefits of both. Created in 1993, these instruments have been widely used by institutional investors (about 75 percent of ETF assets, more than $20 billion in 2001, is held by institutions) and retail investors. ETFs differ from mutual funds because ETFs trade throughout the day and standard mutual funds are priced only at the end of the day. Each ETF trade carries brokerage fees, but their expense ratios are low. They can be bought on margin, there are no investment minimums, and you are unlikely to inherit capital gains from earlier investors. But just like traditional stock investments, remember the 80-20 rule. Over long periods you can expect only 20 percent of investors will benefit by deviating from a buy-and-hold strategy and 80 percent will not.

39

ETHICS OF FINANCIAL PLANNING

The U.S. Constitution guarantees freedom of religion and Americans participate in a variety of faiths. When the nation was formed, the founding fathers were profoundly influenced by their reading of the Bible and by a Judeo-Christian tradition that dates back over 3,000 years. That tradition, and indeed all major organized religions, have sought to define the ethical duties of men and women in terms of their personal and social responsibilities. Duty, honesty, moral standards, and principles are recommended by every religious tradition, and their systems of values form the basis of every society and economic system. Ethics are instrumental in establishing the trust and confidence that make business possible. No intelligent person would do business with someone they know to be unethical or dishonest, and wealth gained by unethical means is always insecure and subject to forfeiture or loss.

The Judeo-Christian tradition defines five ethical uses for money: giving, repaying debts, paying taxes, providing for one's family, and planning for future needs. All of these activities require wise money management and financial planning. In practicing these uses of money, one should feel that his or her actions are carrying out one's ethical duties and not merely pursuing one's own self-interest.

1. Giving. Americans are among the most generous people in the world, and IRS figures reveal that low-income Americans give as much to charity as those in high-income brackets. The recipients include churches, schools, and other nonprofit organizations, which provide valuable services to the society at large. The Bible says it is more blessed to give than to receive (Acts 20:35), and by including planned giving in your budget, you are able to help others on a regular basis and enjoy the personal satisfaction of knowing you can live on less than you earn. Moreover, research has shown that people who focus on the needs of others are happier than those who think only of themselves.

2. Repaying debts. While debt should be avoided, it is sometimes necessary to finance the purchase of a major item such as a home or a car. If people could not be trusted to repay their debts, then there would be no credit available and the whole economy would be drastically affected. In the Bible it says that the wicked borrow and do not repay (Psalms 37:21). Repaying one's debts helps ensure that credit is available to others and allows society as a whole to enjoy a higher standard of living. It also enhances one's credit rating and ensures that credit will be available if needed in the future.

3. Paying taxes. When asked if it was ethical to pay taxes to the pagan Roman empire, Jesus advised his hearers to render unto Caesar that which is Caesar's (Matthew 22:21). The Judeo-Christian tradition has always held it proper to support the legitimate governments and magistrates of this world and to bear a portion of the overall social responsibility. Without tax revenues, governments could not function, and programs such as national defense, aid to the poor, maintenance of the transportation system, public education, and repayment of the public debt would all come to a halt. Society benefits from all these government activities, and you benefit from meeting your social responsibilities and fulfilling your ethical duties. On the other hand, failure to pay the proper amount of taxes may result in penalties and interest charges, and tax evasion is a criminal offense.

4. Providing for one's family. This is a basic moral obligation, and the Bible applauds the wise woman who watches over the affairs of her household (Proverbs 31:27). Thoughtful financial planning enables a family to identify worthwhile financial objectives and to facilitate their accomplishment. If individuals fail to provide for their families, society as a whole suffers, both from the burden of supporting more people and from the effects of such examples of financial irresponsibility. Many social problems, such as the high proportion of women and children living in poverty, child abuse, teenage gang activity, and crime in general, have grown out of the failure of individuals to provide for their own families.

5. Planning for future needs. Saving for a rainy day and investing wisely are considered morally worthy actions in Judeo-Christian ethics. The Bible speaks of the wise woman who "considers a field and buys it; out of her earnings she plants a vineyard" (Proverbs 31:16). Saving should be a component in everyone's budget. Long-term financial planning includes setting aside funds on a regular basis to provide for future needs such as retirement or children's college expenses. Savings are also necessary to meet unexpected financial demands such as home or car repairs.

Managing money wisely is personally rewarding. Good money management will enable you to meet your family's financial needs as well as to help others. You will be able to enhance your children's lives, not merely by giving them things, but by teaching them through example how to handle money.

Almost everyone knows that riches do not bring lasting happiness. In the Bible it says that whoever loves money never has enough money and that whoever loves wealth is never satisfied with his income (Ecclesiastes

5:10). There is a crucial distinction, however, between loving money and managing money wisely. Accumulating wealth for no reason but to be rich would be utter foolishness, but managing money to accomplish appropriate goals and objectives is true wisdom.

40

KEEP MONEY IN PERSPECTIVE

Everyone has heard the old adage that *money can't buy everything*. Virtually everyone agrees that the people in our lives are more important than money. On the other hand, how many people occasionally place their jobs ahead of their spouses, children, relatives, and friends? Where you spend your time is the true indicator of what you value most. Workaholics often lose track of their priorities. Anyone who sacrifices important personal relationships for career or monetary advancement has made a tragic error in judgment.

At the end of life, has anyone ever looked back and said, "I wish I had spent two more hours each day at work?" Certainly not! Regrets usually involve the paucity of time spent with aging parents, children, and spouses. Remember that money is merely a means to an end, not an end in itself. Money is required for the acquisition of food, clothing, shelter, and other necessary items. If you have a lot of money, then you can purchase nonessential items, such as caviar for food, mink coats for clothing, and large mansions for housing. However, no matter how rich you are, you will never have more than 24 hours a day to live. Everyone is equally poor or rich in that regard. How you spend your time is ultimately connected to how truly successful you are. Managing your money wisely will enable you to spend your time in a more useful manner, such as with family and friends.

Don't waste your time or your money! A primary advantage of good financial planning is that the money you make will be used more efficiently. And if your money is more efficiently used, then you can work fewer hours to achieve the same quality of life than if your money is not efficiently used. Set realistic financial goals that can be achieved without sacrificing important personal relationships.

If you are married, then you already know that for financial planning to succeed, it must be done with your spouse. Building a good marriage requires spending time with your spouse, and part of that time should focus on financial planning. Spending time together is essential for a couple to remain close; good financial planning will enable you to spend more time together as a married couple without worrying about finances. A major cause of marital problems is disagreement over money—not necessarily lack of it, but how it is spent. If you are married, spend some time right now with your spouse discussing financial goals and objectives.

Agreement between spouses on goals and objectives is usually essential for financial and marital success. Your goals don't have to be identical to those of your mate, but there should be some common items. For example, you may both wish to save for an expensive vacation together or, if you have children, for college tuition. Working together for common goals is also a way to strengthen your marriage. Of course, not all goals need be held in common; each partner may have individual goals to pursue as well.

Personal financial planning revolves around your entire family. You must teach your children about money and consult older children when making financial decisions that have an impact on them. Let your children know early if you cannot afford to send them to an expensive private university. Your estate plan should be known to your adult children.

If you are a parent, then you know that children don't really care how much money you make, though that indifference doesn't keep them from pleading for the latest toy craze. What children truly care about is how much time you spend with them. Don't believe in that myth called "quality time." Children, especially small ones, can't distinguish between quantity and quality of time. Your children would rather have more time with you than a bigger house, a nicer car, or even the latest toy. If you don't believe this, think back to your own childhood. What is it you most enjoy remembering about those years?

As with relationships with spouses and children, relationships with relatives and friends also require a time commitment if they are to deepen. These associations, while not as critical as those with a spouse or children, are nonetheless important. Good financial planning will enable you to spend more time doing things that give you the greatest satisfaction, such as developing friendships. If you are financially successful, you may even have the opportunity to assist a friend financially. A good point to remember here is that if you can afford to lend money to a financially troubled friend, you can probably afford to give it outright. Loans cause stress between even the best of friends.

QUESTIONS AND ANSWERS

Q. What is diversification?

A. Diversification is an investment strategy for reducing risk. Diversification is the allocation of your investment dollars among different types of investment vehicles and institutions (such as real estate, growth stocks, income stocks, bank certificate of deposits, precious metals). Consequently, your risk exposure is not limited to only one market condition. Having a "balanced portfolio" means that your investments are adequately diversified.

Q. What is a cash equivalent?

A. A cash equivalent is the cash value of an investment. For example, the cash value of a U.S. savings bond is less than its face value (maturity value) on the day you purchase it. For a Series EE bond, the purchase price or cash equivalent is one half of its face value. As interest accrues on the bond, its cash equivalent value increases. A savings bond can be readily converted to cash. Some people refer to assets that can be readily converted to cash as "cash equivalents," although any asset has a cash equivalent value.

Q. What is liquidity?

A. Liquidity indicates how quickly and efficiently an asset can be converted to cash without losing any of the amount originally invested. For example, a passbook savings account can be immediately converted to cash. It is a true cash equivalent. A bank certificate of deposit (CD) also can be quickly converted to cash, but there is usually an early withdrawal penalty. Thus, a bank CD is not 100 percent liquid because of this withdrawal penalty. Real estate investments are even less liquid. The owner must first find a buyer before cash can be obtained from the investment. Generally, an investor expects a higher return from less liquid investments because liquidity is related to the level of risk. Risk is the main determinant of the level of return on an investment. Less liquidity may mean that more time is required to find a buyer and sell the investment; this time factor often means great risk.

Q. What is a balance sheet?

A. A balance sheet shows the total assets, total liabilities (debts), and total equity (net worth) of a business or an individual. The balance sheet of an individual is referred to as a personal balance sheet and is the starting point of personal financial planning. A balance sheet is a snapshot of your financial standing at a given point in time.

Q. What is an income statement?

A. An income statement shows the income, expenses, and net income of an individual or a business. The value of a company as an investment depends largely on the firm's future profits (net income). Stock market listings typically show the firm's price/earnings ratio, which is the current market value of a share of stock divided by the company's earnings per share (EPS). EPS is computed by dividing the company's net income by the number of outstanding shares of stock. A personal income statement shows your net income or loss for the year in question.

Q. What are financial statements?

A. Financial statements for businesses include the balance sheet, income statement, statement of cash flows, and statement of retained earnings (which may be incorporated into the balance sheet).

The *balance sheet* shows the financial position of an entity (or person) at a specific point in time.

The *income statement* shows the net income (revenues minus expenses) of an entity for a specific period of time.

The *statement of cash flows* depicts the cash inflows and outflows for a specific period of time. The chief difference between the income statement and the cash flow statement is that revenue and expense items are included on the income statement as they are accrued (incurred), which is not necessarily when cash is received or disbursed. Many small businesses fail not because of lack of profits but because of poor cash flow.

The *statement of retained earnings* shows the change in retained earnings of a company from the beginning of a period (for instance, January 1) to the end of the period (for instance, December 31). In general, retained earnings are increased by net income—or decreased by net loss—and are decreased by dividends. Basically, a firm can either retain its earnings (net income) to expand its operations or pay out its earnings as dividends to shareholders.

Q. What is the time horizon?

A. The time horizon, which is frequently affected by your stage in life, is the amount of time you can wait for a particular investment to payoff. Depending on your stage in life, you will have different investment goals and objectives. For example, if you have a six-year-old and you wish to start investing for his or her college education, then your time horizon is 12 years, because in 12 years your child will begin college. If you are 35 years old and plan to retire at age 65, then your time horizon is 30 years. The investments in the college fund must begin paying off in 12 years, while the investments in the retirement fund must begin paying off in 30 years.

Q. What is a tax shelter?

A. A tax shelter is an investment that provides a tax advantage, such as special tax deductions or exemptions. For example, interest income from municipal bonds is usually exempt from federal income tax. The interest expense associated with a home mortgage is tax deductible. Tax law often provides for tax shelters to encourage Americans to make investments to further certain national economic goals. Assisting state and local governments to raise money through bond issues (by exempting interest on such bonds from federal income tax) is considered beneficial to the nation in general. Thus, the tax shelter of tax-exempt bonds was incorporated into the federal tax laws. The same rationale applies to the encouragement of individual home ownership by permitting a deduction for mortgage interest.

Q. How much risk should an individual accept?

A. Risk should be directly connected to the investment's potential return. A bank CD may not pay the highest return, but it also offers virtually no risk. You are guaranteed a certain return (for example, 5 percent) on your investment. Furthermore, it is highly liquid. At the other extreme is a speculative stock issue. The stock price may increase or decrease, depending on the company's performance. In a worst-case scenario, the company might even go out of business, wiping out your investment.

Never make an investment if you are uncomfortable with the risk involved. Some people are bigger risk takers than others. If you are a risk-averse person, you might even jeopardize your health by losing sleep over a high-risk investment. If so, you would probably be better off settling for a lesser return on a lower-risk investment. In general, the more money people have, the less risk they tend to take with their investments. That may be the way many people became wealthy in the first place.

Q. What is an envelope budget?

A. An envelope budget is a simple but effective budgeting system that works in spite of a lack of financial discipline. You take envelopes and write the name of each of your expenditures on them (such as car payment, house payment, food). At the beginning of each month when you receive your paycheck, write checks for each of the envelopes.

You mail the house payment and car payment checks to the lenders. You also mail the checks for the utility and telephone bills. The other checks are cashed when payments are required and the cash is used to buy gas, food, and necessities. Any cash left over after the first purchase is replaced in the appropriate envelope. Any amount remaining at the end of the month is transferred to your savings and investment envelope. Thanks to the envelope system, you know how much you have left to spend for any item in your budget at any given time. As a result, you take control of your finances and are successfully achieving your financial goals. The major advantage of the envelope approach to budgeting is that it physically divides funds among your individual budget items. Additionally, it allows you to readily ascertain the status of any budget item—what funds are currently available for each item.

Q. How do you check your credit rating?

A. To check your credit rating, you must contact one or more of the credit bureaus that maintain your credit report. There are over 2,000 credit bureaus across the country; a few of the largest are Trans Union, TRW, Chilton, CBI, and Associated Credit Services. Most credit bureaus charge a small fee, such as $10, to provide you with a copy of your credit report. The report does not actually give a credit rating, but provides a selective listing of your employment and credit history. For example, the report lists the name, number, type, and activity of credit cards issued in your name, the time you have had these cards, and the outstanding balances on each card. Sometimes mistakes are made. If you find an error on your credit report, you should notify the credit bureau immediately.

Q. Where do you obtain tax forms and IRS publications?

A. The IRS provides tax forms and helpful publications free of charge to taxpayers. Many banks, post offices, and libraries have the basic forms available. A complete list of IRS publications is provided in Publication 910, which, along with other forms and publications, can be requested from the Forms Distribution Center for your state. Also, many libraries make available copies of forms and publications that you can photocopy. Publication 17, "Your Federal Income Tax," is particularly helpful for tax return preparation.

Q. How do you open a brokerage account for buying and selling stock?

A. To open a brokerage account, you must provide your name, address, occupation, Social Security number, citizenship, a suitable bank or financial reference, and an acknowledgment that you are of legal age. There are a number of online brokers available to investors. Most people open "cash accounts," meaning that they will settle transactions promptly without credit. "Margin accounts" are used by customers who wish to use borrowed funds to supplement their own commitment. In this case, the investor makes only partial payment for the securities and borrows the rest from a broker. Margin accounts are better suited to more experienced investors who are prepared to assume additional risks.

Q. What are financial ratios?

A. Financial ratios assist investors in determining the financial strength of a potential investment. Analysts use many financial ratios. Some of the most prominent ones are based on amounts reported in a firm's income statement. Some of the best-known ratios using income statement values are as follows:

1. Profit margin is computed by dividing net income (profit) by net sales for the period. The equation for this ratio is:

$$\text{Profit margin on sales} = \frac{\text{Net Income}}{\text{Net sales}}$$

   This ratio indicates the ability of the company to generate profits through sales to customers.

2. Return on common stock is the ultimate measure of operating success to owners. It is computed by dividing net income less preferred dividends by the equity of common stockholders. In equation form:

$$\text{Rate of return on common stock equity}$$
$$= \frac{\text{Net income} - \text{preferred dividends}}{\text{Common stockholders' equity}}$$

   In determining common stockholders' equity, it is necessary to subtract from total stockholders' equity the stockholders' equity that pertains to preferred stock.

3. Price/earnings ratio is widely used by analysts in assessing the investment possibilities of different stocks. It is calculated by dividing the market price of the stock by the earnings per share:

$$\text{P/E ratio} = \frac{\text{Market price of stock}}{\text{Earnings per share}}$$

High P/E stocks are typically associated with greater growth potential than low P/E stocks.

4. Payout ratio is the ratio of cash dividends to net income.

$$\text{Payout ratio} = \frac{\text{Dividends per share}}{\text{Earnings per share}}$$

Many investors prefer securities with a fairly substantial payout ratio. Other investors are more concerned with growth in sales and profits, which leads to appreciation in the price of the stock. By contrast, utility companies often have a high payout ratio. High-growth companies tend to have low payout ratios because they reinvest most of their earnings.

Q. Where can I find information about mutual funds?

A. *Barron's* publishes special mutual fund surveys quarterly in mid-February, May, August, and November, including articles and performance statistics. *Forbes* publishes a highly regarded survey in August or September and features ten-year performance records of all funds, a selective "honor roll" of outstanding funds, and a ranking of how funds have performed in rising and falling markets. In February of each year, *Business Week* publishes ratings of mutual funds that weigh five years of total returns against the risks taken to make those returns. Finally, *Money* publishes regular articles about mutual funds and extensive quarterly statistics on performance.

Q. What is net asset value (NAV) per share?

A. NAV refers to the price at which an open-end mutual fund sells or redeems its shares, less any redemption or deferred sales charges. This figure is calculated each day by deducting the fund's total liabilities from its total assets, then dividing the resulting amount by the number of outstanding shares.

Q. What protection does my stock portfolio have with a stock broker?

A. Your brokerage accounts are insured by as much as $500,000 by the Securities Investor Protection Corporation (SIPC). But this protection covers only losses due to theft and proven unauthorized trading. Such things as fraud, excessive trading, and manipulation of stock prices do not qualify. Plus you cannot sue your broker because you agree to take any disputes to arbitration. Apparently, only about 55 percent of disputes heard by arbitrators are decided in favor of investors. Check out brokers at *www.nasdr.com* and *www.nasdadr.com*.

Q. What is the difference between a limited liability company (LLC) and a limited liability partnership (LLP)?

A. These forms of business organization are available in at least 36 states. Both forms may be taxed like a partnership, but the limited liability company (LLC) is taxed by state franchise taxes. The LLC provides limited liability to all partners, but an LLP partner remains personally liable for his or her own negligence or misdeeds.

Q. What is the difference between an active mutual fund and an indexed mutual fund?

A. Active funds are managed by professional advisors who pick stocks they believe to have the greatest potential. These funds hope to beat the Standard & Poor's 500 Index or the Wilshire 5000 Index. Indexed funds, on the other hand, seek to perform exactly equal to a stock market index, and these passively managed funds can outperform many of the active funds.

Q. What is franchising?

A. In addition to building a business and using the annuity concept, franchising is another wealth-building strategy. A private franchise is a contract for the exclusive right to perform certain functions or to sell certain products or services. Some well-known franchises include McDonalds, Jiffy-Lube, Dairy Queen, Burger King, and Subway. The key to such agreements is the use by the franchisee of the trademark, trade name, patent, process, recipe, or know-how of the franchiser for the term of the franchise.

Franchises may be granted by individuals, corporations, or governmental units. A public utility is granted a perpetual, indeterminate, or indefinitely terminable franchise by the community it serves.

Q. What is arbitraging?

A. Arbitrage refers to the process of taking advantage of the difference in price that similar assets may be worth at the same time in different places. This approach can be a powerful way to accumulate wealth.

For any purchase, you should try to buy low and sell high. An arbitrager buys and sells at known present prices in different places and makes money without taking a risk. The shorter the time period between the purchase and sale, the less risk there is. Of course, not all arbitrage is risk-free, but you should look for significant price disequilibria in any type of asset.

Technically, arbitrage refers to the system of equalizing prices in different commercial centers by buying in the cheaper market and selling in the higher market. Eventually, arbitrage levels prices and causes equilibrium.

GLOSSARY

Accounting Tax Records taxpayer's regular books of account and such other records and data as may be necessary to support the entries on his or her books of account and tax return.

Actuary professional insurance statistician who calculates risk, premiums, insurance costs, and related matters.

ADRs (American Depository Receipts) negotiable receipts representing ownership of stock in a foreign corporation traded on an exchange.

AICPA professional organization of certified public accountants, called the American Institute of CPAs.

Alternative Minimum Tax additional tax to ensure that taxpayers approaching $100,000 of taxable income pay at least a minimum tax.

A.M. Best & Company independent firm that rates annuities, insurance companies, and so on.

Annual report formal financial statement issued yearly by a company.

Annuitant individual who enters a contract to set up an annuity.

Annuity agreement between a client and an insurance company, in which, for a lump-sum payment, the company agrees to pay the client a lump payment or periodic payments starting at some future date (for instance, at retirement). *See* Variable and Fixed-rate Annuity.

Arbitrage strategy to profit from differences in the price of the same investment that is traded in two or more markets.

Asset economic resource expected to provide future benefits to a person or company.

At-risk Rules tax provisions that limit the amount of tax losses an investor can deduct.

Back-end Load charge or exit fee you must pay when you sell your mutual fund shares.

Balance Sheet financial statement that provides information about the assets, liabilities, and owners' equity of a company or individual as of a particular date.

Bear Market period of falling stock prices.

Beneficiary person who is entitled to the benefits from trust property or who inherits under a will.

Beta indicates a security's or mutual fund's volatility relative to that of the market itself.

Bid current purchase price of a stock less the dealer's markup or spread.

Blue Chip well-known company with a proven record of profits and a long history of dividend payments.

Bond Ratings system of evaluating the credit quality of bonds by assigning the bonds to different risk classifications.

Budget plan to control income and expenses.

Bull Market period of rising stock prices.

Business Risk unsystematic risk involving the possibility that cash flow is inadequate to sustain a business enterprise.

Cafeteria Benefit Plan type of pension plan that allows employees to contribute as much as 15 percent of their annual salary up to a maximum of $11,000 in 2002.

Call Option right, but not an obligation, to purchase 100 shares of a stock or market index at a set price prior to a deadline.

Callable Bond one that can be retired prematurely by the issuer for a specified payment, which is usually slightly above the face value.

Capitalization market value of a corporation, which is determined by multiplying the total number of shares by the per-share price.

Cash Flow dividends, interest payments, realized profits, and any other return from an investment.

Cash Surrender Value amount that a policy owner is entitled to receive if coverage is discontinued.

CATS zero-coupon bonds issued by the United States government, called Certificates of Accrual on Treasury Securities.

Certified Financial Planner designation given by the College for Financial Planning to individuals who successfully complete a five-course curriculum.

Charitable Remainder Annuity Trust trust that is to pay its income beneficiary (or beneficiaries) a specific sum that is not less than 5 percent of the initial fair market value of all property placed in the trust.

Charitable Remainder Unitrust trust that is to pay the income beneficiary (or beneficiaries) a fixed percentage that is not less than 5 percent of the net fair market value of its assets (as valued annually).

Charitable Trust trust originated in an effort to make one or more gifts to a charitable organization.

Closed-end Mutual Fund fund that issues a fixed number of shares.

Codicil amendment to a will.

Commodity Futures agreement to purchase or sell a specific amount of a commodity at a particular price on a stipulated future date.

Common Stock fractional shares of ownership interest in a corporation.

Community Property property acquired during marriage in certain states such as Alaska, Arizona, California, Idaho, Louisiana, Nevada, New Mexico, Texas, Washington, and Wisconsin, whereby the law presumes the property to be the product of joint efforts. Thus, in a divorce the couple's total property is divided in half, unless a negotiated settlement is reached, even if most of the assets were earned by one member of the couple.

Compound Interest interest that is computed on principal plus interest accrued during a previous period or periods.

Convertible Security bond or share of preferred stock that can be exchanged into a specified amount of common stock at a specified price.

Corpus term used for the principal of a trust.

Currency Transaction Reports (CTRs) banks are required to file with the Treasury Department a report for currency transactions exceeding $10,000.

Decedent dead person.

Defined Benefit Plan retirement plan that allows an employee to select the amount of retirement benefits that will be received.

Defined Contribution Plan type of retirement plan in which the amount of the employer's contributions are fixed, but the amount of the employee's pension is not.

Diamonds index fund that trades on the AMEX and tracks the Dow Jones Industrial Average.

Diversification spreading investments among a number of different securities to reduce the risk inherent in investing.

Dollar Cost Averaging system of buying an investment at regular intervals with a fixed dollar amount.

Donee person receiving a gift.

Donor person making a gift.

Estate Planning art of designing a program for the effective enjoyment, management, and disposition of property at the minimum possible tax cost.

Estate Tax tax imposed on the fair market value of all assets less liabilities held by a person at death.

Exchange Traded Fund (ETF) hybrid of stocks and indexed mutual funds that allows investors to invest in a diversified portfolio.

Executor or Executrix person designated by will to manage the assets and liabilities of the decedent.

Financial Ratios indicators of a company's financial performance and position.

Financial Risk unsystematic risk involving the possibility that cash flow is insufficient to service debt used to finance the business.

Fixed-rate Annuity annuity that guarantees a rate of return for a specific period of time (such as one or five years). *See* Annuity and Variable-rate Annuity.

Franchise right or privilege conferred by law.

Fraud (Tax) willful intent by a taxpayer to evade the assessment of a tax. IRS bears the burden of proof.

Futures Contract legal contract to buy or sell a standardized quantity of a commodity or a standardized financial instrument at a specified future date and price.

Gift Tax excise tax imposed on the transfer of a taxable amount of property during life or upon death.

Ginnie Maes (GNMA) mortgage-backed securities.

Grantor Lead Trust trust in which the income from property is paid to a grantor for a period of years and the remainder accrues to a younger-generation beneficiary.

Grantor Trust trust under which the grantor retains the right to the income for life. After the grantor's death the remainder goes to the beneficiary (or beneficiaries). This type of trust cannot be revoked.

Hard Assets tangible investments such as gold, silver, rare coins, stamps, art, and gems.

Holographic Will will in one's own handwriting.

"I Love You" Will will tailored to married couples with small estates in which all assets are left to the surviving spouse.

Income Statement financial statement that shows a firm's revenues and expenses over a period of time.

Index Funds mutual fund with a portfolio designed to track a broad based index (such as Wilshire 5000).

Interest Rate rate charged for the use of money.

Interest Rate Risk systematic risk involving the probability that an investment's value will vary in response to a change in market interest rates.

Intestate having made no will; used to identify a situation in which a person dies without a will.

IRA individual retirement account, a tax-deferred

retirement plan for certain individuals with earned income, which allows a deduction for contributions.

Irrevocable Trust trust agreement that cannot be revoked and usually cannot be changed or modified.

Joint Tenancy joint control over the property or interest during the lifetime of the tenants. Upon the death of a joint tenant, such interest passes automatically to the surviving joint tenant.

Joint Venture agreement between two or more parties to invest in a piece of property or a business.

Junk Bond high-risk bond with a credit rating of BB or lower.

Keogh Plan tax-deferred retirement plan available to self-employed individuals.

Liabilities economic obligations of a person to outsiders.

Leverage accelerative effect of debt on financial returns.

Life Insurance Trust use of a trust for the disposition of life insurance proceeds. This type of trust has become a significant part of estate planning.

Limited Partnership type of partnership in which some of the partners have limited liability.

Liquidity ease with which an asset can be converted into cash.

Living Trust revocable trust used to avoid probate, to avoid having assets on public record, and to reduce the time the assets are frozen.

Load Fund type of mutual fund in which the buyer must pay a sales fee, or commission, on top of the price.

Margin in securities, the amount of cash down payment and money borrowed from a broker to purchase stocks; in futures, a deposit of money that can be used by the broker to cover losses that may occur in trading futures.

Marital Deduction deduction available to the surviving spouse of a decedent. Only the net amount of property that passes to the surviving spouse is allowed as a marital deduction. This deduction is also available to arrive at a value for taxable gifts of property given to a spouse.

Market Makers securities dealers who help set bid and asked prices for a stock by standing ready to buy and sell shares at quoted prices.

Market Risk systematic risk resulting from the tendency of the price of an investment to rise and fall in value in conjunction with the market as a whole.

Municipal Bond tax-exempt security issued by state and local governments and local government agencies and authorities.

Mutual Funds pool of funds, contributed by investors, which is used to purchase a number of securities. The mutual fund is managed by professional managers for a fee.

Naked Call risky option position, in which one sells a call, to earn the premium income without owning the underlying security.

Net Worth the result of subtracting what you owe from what you own.

No-load Fund type of mutual fund for which no fee is charged when shares are purchased.

Nonmarital Trust trust that is created for the purpose of avoiding taxation on the exemption equivalent amount ($1,000,000).

Nonrecourse Loan loans in which the lender has no recourse against the borrower's personal assets in the event of the borrower's default.

Numismatics study of coins.

Nuncupative Will oral will that is generally not held to be valid.

Open-end Mutual Fund fund that issues additional shares to meet investor demand to purchase more shares at a price equal to net asset value.

Over-the-counter Market market that trades securities through a centralized computer telephone network that links dealers across the United States.

Partnership agreement between two or more associates to enter into business or to invest in assets. A partnership is a flow-through entity and pays no taxes.

Penny Stock relatively low-priced speculative stock.

Philately study of postage stamps.

Pink Sheets daily listings of over-the-counter stocks and their market makers, named for the color of paper used for the lists.

Power of Attorney written instrument by which people appoint an attorney-in-fact to act as their agent and give him or her the authority to act in their behalf.

Prenuptial Agreement contract between prospective spouses in which they outline mutual promises concerning their respective rights after marriage. It is increasingly used in second marriages and marriages in later life.

Private Annuity arrangement in which a transferor transfers property to a transferee in exchange for the transferee's unsecured promise to make periodic payments for the remainder of the transferor's life.

Probate Assets those assets in an estate that are subject to probate and court disposition and thus become part of public records.

Prospectus official written contract for buying a mutual fund, outlining its objectives, risks, expenses, and management.

Purchasing Power Risk systematic risk resulting from the impact of inflation or deflation on an investment.

Put Option right, but not an obligation, to sell 100 shares of a stock or market index at a set price prior to a deadline.

Real Estate Investment Trust (REIT) entity similar to a mutual fund that invests in real estate rather than stocks and bonds.

Recourse Loan lender has recourse against the property pledged and against the borrower's personal assets (subject to local statutes) in the event of the borrower's default on a loan.

Revocable Inter Vivos Trust trust created during the settlor's lifetime, which the settlor alone has the power to revoke and in which the effect of the revocation is to force the return of the corpus to the settlor.

Risk Management identification and measurement of risk exposures and decisions on how to handle the identified risks.

Risk Tolerance ability of a person to tolerate risk and remain undisturbed in the face of changes in the value of investment holdings.

Roth IRA type of tax-deferred IRA that does not allow a deduction for contributions, but later distributions may be tax-free.

Schedule C tax form schedule that a person uses for each business; also used by self-employed persons. It lists business income less expenses.

S corporation corporation with 75 or fewer shareholders that elects not to be taxed like a regular corporation. The corporate income and expenses flow through to the shareholders based upon their ownership interests.

Sector Fund mutual fund that invests in one industry or segment of the economy (for example, gold mining).

Settlor person in a trust relationship who creates or intentionally causes the trust to come into existence. Other terms used to designate this person include donor, trustor, and grantor.

Single-state Fund bond fund that holds municipal bonds issued by government entities within a specified geographical area. Bonds purchased by residents of the issuing state are generally exempt from federal, state, and local income taxes.

Special Agent member of the Criminal Investigation Division of the IRS, the sole objective of which is to develop a criminal case against taxpayers.

Spiders index product that tracks Standard & Poor's 500 stock Index and is traded on the AMEX.

Standard Deviation volatility indicator that represents a probable range in which a security or mutual fund's price might move, based on information calculated over preceding years. The greater the standard deviation, the greater the variability and the greater the total investment risk.

Statement of Cash Flows financial statement that shows a firm's cash receipts and cash payments over a period of time.

STRIPS zero-coupon bond issued by the U.S. government with separate trading of the interest and principal portions of securities.

Support Trust trust that is designed to provide support for the beneficiary.

Systematic Risk investment risk that results from economic, political, and sociological factors, including market changes, interest rate fluctuations, and purchasing power risks.

Tax Avoidance tax reduction methods permitted by law.

Tax Evasion any method of reducing taxes not permitted by law. Tax evasion involves deceit, subterfuge, camouflage, concealment, or an attempt to color or obscure events; it carries heavy penalties.

Tax Shelter investment that produces after-tax income that is greater than before-tax income. Such an investment may provide before-tax cash flow that generates losses to shield other income from taxation.

Tenancy by the Entirety form of property ownership by married couples whereby upon death one spouse's interest is automatically transferred to the other spouse. You may not sell or give away your share without obtaining permission from your spouse.

Tenants in Common form of property ownership where upon death your share of the property goes to heirs named in your will.

Term Insurance pure death protection that does not include a savings element.

Testamentary term given to a trust created at the death of the decedent.

Three-part Will will in which some assets pass directly to the spouse, some property goes into a bypass trust, and the remainder passes to a qualified terminable interest property trust.

TIGRS zero-coupon bond issued by the U.S. government called Treasury Investment Growth Receipts.

Treasury Securities debt obligations issued by the U.S. government and backed by its faith and credit.

Trust fiduciary relationship in which one party holds property subject to an equitable obligation to keep or use such property for the benefit of another person.

Trustee person who holds the legal title to the trust property for the benefit of the beneficiary.

Trust Property interest in a thing—real or personal, tangible or intangible—that the trustee holds, subject to the rights of another.

Two-part Will will in which some assets pass directly to the surviving spouse while the remaining assets are deposited in a bypass trust.

Unit Investment Trust (UIT) "dumb" mutual fund in which a set number of units are sold, and one purchases units for, say, $1,000 each. There is no active management, and some of the bonds may be called early.

Unsystematic Risk risk associated with the nature of a business enterprise underlying the investment, which includes business and financial risk.

Variable-rate Annuity annuity that provides possible high yields because investments are chosen as often as once a month. *See* Annuity and Fixed-rate Annuity.

Will legal document that serves as a key vehicle of property transfer at death. Within the document are specific instructions concerning the disposition of the estate and naming the designated executor (executrix).

Zero-coupon Municipal Bond bond that is purchased at deep discount off the face value. It offers no semiannual interest, and full face value is paid at maturity. The interest coupon is stripped from the principal portion. The longer the maturity, the higher the yield.

INDEX

BARRON'S BUSINESS KEYS

Each "key" explains approximately 50 concepts and provides a glossary and index. Each book: Paperback, approx. 160 pp., 4³/₁₆" x 7", $4.95, $5.95, & $7.95 Can. $6.50, $7.95, $8.50, & $11.50.

Barron's Educational Series, Inc.
250 Wireless Boulevard • Hauppauge, NY 11788
In Canada: Georgetown Book Warehouse
34 Armstrong Avenue, Georgetown, Ont. L7G 4R9
www.barronseduc.com

(#10) R 1/02